Copyright © 2022   Shawn Wallis
All rights reserved.

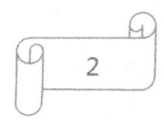

Flight of the Mockingbird

By
Shawn Wallis

"The fearless mockingbird defends its nest and territory, diving at and attacking predators and those who come too close. They teach us to develop self-confidence, to speak our truth and stand up for what is ours by right."

-Harper Lee

"Shawn, I need you these next two years. You are more than capable of leading us defensively, but I can't in any way put you in the lineup. I could lose my job, benefits, pension, and even my family. I am sorry, but if you choose to walk away, then so be it. I can't stop you. You have an unbelievable talent, and I would hate to see you throw it away, despite my reluctance. I think what is best for you is to remain on the bump and hammer out these wins for us. I know what you are capable of in the batter's box, but this team needs a leader on the mound. If you want to walk away at the end of the season, I can't stop you."

- Coach Dick Sauchuk
Masconomet Baseball
March 3^{d}, 1990

Table of Contents

Introduction

Chapter 1   Shadow of the Paragon

Chapter 2   Stairway to Hell

Chapter 3   The River of Darkness

Chapter 4   Next to Nothing

Chapter 5   Feed the Wolf

Chapter 6   My Own Prison

Chapter 7   The Darkness Settles in...

Chapter 8   The Cult of Personality

Chapter 9   Indemnification

Chapter 10   Night of the Hunter

Chapter 11   A Beautiful Lie

Chapter 12   The Perfect Weapon

Chapter 13   Pulse of the Maggots

Letter from the Author

Introduction

In early January of 1987, a tragic crime of violence penetrates the shores of the Red River in South Boston. Until now, this horrific secret would shatter the small town of Weymouth and transform the residents beneath a dark cloud of suspicion and misery. Months later, a teen and his mother would walk upon the doors of Masconomet High School and apply for enrollment. Unaware of the teen's life-long tragedies, the brittle boy is welcomed with open arms among the society of radical thoughts and gripping wealth. The small town twenty-one miles north of Boston would attempt to blanket the sacrifice of a mockingbird's silence, only to awaken a demon amid the hollow of his shadow. Can the determination of one teen calm the waters from the river of darkness, or will he succumb to the fruits of his tormentors. Welcome yourself to the amazing true story from the hallways of Masconomet and the miraculous flight of the mockingbird.

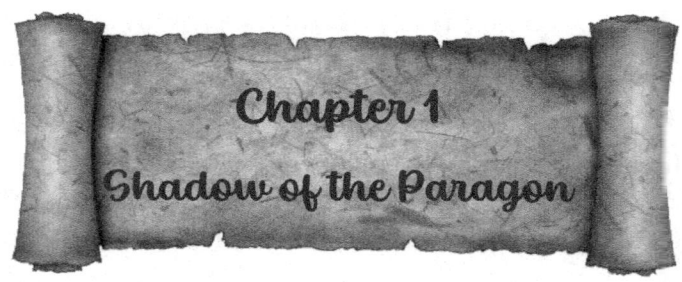

Chapter 1
Shadow of the Paragon

On a warm day in July of 1994, the sun begins to set upon the small town of Lynn, Massachusetts. Several people are setting their eyes upon the man swinging his bat inside of the on-deck circle. The stadium bear witness to a phenomenon like no other as the whispers among the crowd overshadowed their curiosity. The back end of the double header produced statstics unseen in any semi-professional ball player in decades, and the town's people took immediate notice. The brightness of the park's lights attempts to unravel the spirit of the opposing team, but no answer could be given for the riddle of the new stranger. His name is Alexander to his teammates, and he is a transient passing through town, seeking solace in a summer of baseball. His reluctance to speak about his past temper expectations surrounding the young man, but his presence uplifts his team to victory. The beautiful stranger stood a solid inch below six foot and he barely weighed one hundred and eighty pounds. His glowing blue eyes and short brown hair blend smartly within his pale complexion. The softness of his voice brings others to maintain a plethora of conversations about the game of baseball. Unaware of his age, many guess in their minds the perfect stranger was barely twenty years old. He reminded them of a character from the movie *"The Natural"* and his energy brought together an unlikely number of wins on the young season. The man without a history was the talk of the Boston area and tonight's games brought forward a pair of curious eyes to the forefront of this unsolved mystery. Three friends were sitting on the bleachers and struck up an important conversation.

"Doesn't he look familiar to you guys? I could swear I seen him before", the man with the red Harvard t-shirt asked.

"Who is this guy and how the hell is he not playing for the friggin Red Sox?" The younger man asked.

"How in the world can one man go six for six in game number one and now he is four for four and up at bat already in the sixth inning?" The middleman asked while counting with his fingers.

"I swear to God that is Shawn Wallis out there in that batter's box. Don't you remember him from High School a few years ago? Wasn't he a pitcher?" Jason asked.

"No way Jason. Are you sure?" Doug asked.

The three men placed their hands over their eyes to shade themselves from the bright lights of the stadium. Peeking towards the silhouette of the man standing next to home plate, one of them let out a huge gulp.

"You are right one hundred percent. It looks like Shawn. Oh my god! I just saw him last year coming up to my father's garage and asking for directions. We spoke briefly and he told me that he was venturing up around Topsfield in search of playing baseball. I guess he sort of stuck around", Bill replied.

The friends sat in awe as the stranger stood quietly in the batter's box and swung away at a quick fastball. The smoothness of his swing brough relevance to a prototypical scout and many were watching with angst as the ball sailed clearly over the center field wall.

"Boys. That isn't Shawn Wallis", the voice behind the men stated with confidence.

"Jeff Milks. What are you doing here?" Bill asked as he recognized the man behind him.

"That isn't Shawn. He is somewhere in this world making someone miserable with his countless bullshit and rants. So, believe what you want boys. Shawn left this town many years ago and I recommend you start believing that as well", Jeffrey responded with arrogance.

Watching in awe of the man that used to deliver his electrifying curveball into his mitt, Jeff Milks dazed into the past. Recollecting a time when he was part of a team that made history for his High School, Jeff held his head down for a mere second to gather his thoughts. In his mind, Shawn Wallis was a shadow of the young man that grazed the baseball diamond with ease and accountability. Thoughts of the countless strikeouts and shouting fans grazed Jeff's dignity, but something was missing. How in the world could Shawn be a part of this community and he never knew about it? Why was Shawn here and what made him the man he is today? Jeff asked himself all these questions as he watched his former teammate surround the bases celebrating his long homerun.

"How could we have missed this man's talent all those years ago? How could we have been so wrong on so many levels" Jeff asked himself quietly.

Garnering his thoughts from the past while staring into the lights of the stadium, a familiar voice softened his ears.

"Jeff isn't he beautiful out there", the familiar voice pleasantly mentioned in his left ear.

Looking over his shoulder, the curves of her face endeared her gorgeous voice as he realized the words came from his former love from high school.

"Gretchen Hover? How long has it been?" Jeff asked as he reached out for a hug.

"Jeff, it's been a few years. I see that you found our new surprise out there?" She mentioned.

"How long have you known about Shawn out here?" Jeffrey asked.

"My brother Dan told me about him a month ago. Apparently, Danny has always known Shawn to be a tremendous hitter and I can't understand why you didn't", Gretchen politely mentioned.

Looking into her eyes, Jeff couldn't hold back the lie he had held inside all these years.

"To be honest, I had a lot to do with Shawn being held back that first year. It was Ken Nazarian and Rick Anthony who chimed in on Shawn being relegated all those years ago. We hated him because Rick had lost his starting position on the team, and we could never get it back. Can you believe that Coach Sauchuk picked that piece of shit over Rick? Honesty Gretch, what wasn't to hate? He was obnoxious and cocky, and we couldn't stand him", Jeff chimed in.

"But why Jeff. What was so bad about a teammate that helped your team? Isn't this game about teamwork? Why would you do that to someone? We could have had a championship team for years. Because of you guys, Shawn quit baseball for good after he left Masco our Senior year. Shame on you guys. So, what if Rick lost his position! Shawn never ridiculed Rick and as I recall, weren't they celebrating together when you made the playoffs?" Gretchen asked.

"I was trying to hold him back because he just seemed different. He was always on our nerves, and I couldn't get past the fact that he could have been a better hitter than us. It didn't help

that he lied to the entire school and Principal Smith banned him from the offense. All those days during the summer hearing from my brother Steve and how Shawn was dominating the opposition on his own. This was our team, Gretchen. Our team!", Jeff mentioned.

"I will always love you Jeff, always! But you were an asshole than and you are being an asshole now. I walked away from you because you could have been Shawn's mentor. He needed you and don't you remember what his Father did to him all those years? Shawn's Father was abusive to him mentally, physically and emotionally and he did it in front of all of us. He needed you Jeff and you turned your back on him. Remember when he stayed with you after he was severely beaten, and the cops got involved? Do you remember when he was sexually assaulted by Duane White and his friends in the locker room? Where were you, Jeff? You abandoned him and he moved on and walked away from this amazing game you both love. He lied to the school because he needed help to get away from those bullies. That lie caused Shawn to lose the chance to play in the order and you just allowed it to happen. You could have stood up for him", Gretchen mentioned.

Pausing to gather the recollection of horrible reminders of his past, Jeff cautioned himself to relinquish his pride.

"Don't you think he suffered enough in High School. He was severely bullied and what you all did to him was unforgiveable. Was it worth it to prey on a teenager that was vulnerable? Can you imagine being in his shoes and attempting to make it in a society that didn't want to accept him? He was damaged goods when he walked into our lives, and he left it much worse. Take that pill and swallow it for a moment Jeff and realize the damage you helped create. Don't you recall mentioning to me one night how amazing Shawn was on the mound. What words did you use? Let me think here. Oh, you said: Shawn was a rebel with a golden arm and a doctor of precision with his curveball. Take that for what it is worth and remember one thing. That man out there is a product of a bad Father, bad mentor and horrible coach. Jeff, it was nice seeing you and I wish you well my old friend", Gretchen stated as she walked away in disgust.

Holding his head to his hands, he watched his former love walk away in anger. He sat for the moment and closed his eyes and envisioned a time when things in High School were far from complicated. The echoes from Bill, Jason and Doug's conversation sifted through his brain about the man who everyone was convinced was Shawn Wallis. The man who was perfect on this evening was special to Jeff and he felt sorrow for his horrible decisions. What could Jeff have done differently to allow his old teammate the opportunity to help bring a championship to their High School. Whether it was the near perfect game against North Andover in 1989, the eighteen-strikeout game against Rockport in 1990, or the 15-strikeout game against Stoneham in the playoffs in 1990, life was moving forward regardless.

The chance to make things right stood in front of him and all it would take is a gentle apology to the man he betrayed. Instead of extending an olive branch to his former teammate, Jeff collected himself and walked towards the parking lot. The fact that Shawn was a paragon to a chosen few, Jeff knew his mistakes would have to remain buried. He was a part of a system that was far from perfect and if he chose to rectify his faults, maybe others in the community would hold it against him. Knowing his own failures as a ball player would suffice through a context of bad choices, Jeff remained mute. The countless years of wanting to believe things would have been different if Shawn was given a chance to penetrate the lineup for Masco crept slowly. Sitting in his truck, he began to drive into the darkness of the night. His headlights piercing the roadway, Jeff began to envision the life that was once prominent. Jeff was a valuable baseball prospect for his small college and his thoughts began rambling into the past. What if things were different for him if Shawn had penetrated the lineup and gave Masconomet a powerful offense. Where in the lineup would he have been placed if he had convinced Coach Sauchuk to allow Shawn to play? Where in the field would he have been placed? All the questions came to fruition, and he was left with one reality. Shawn was the great baseball player and friend he needed, but his friends thought otherwise. He relied on his inner circle to propel his pride into something that inflated his ego. He lost Gretchen and the ability to claim two baseball state championships. Was it worth it all to not step in and help save Shawn from his abusive Father? Was it worth watching a teenager lose everything and walk away? For that thought, Jeff had truly respected Shawn and his graceful approach to the game of Baseball. Secretly, he respected what he was able to attain and accomplish in a short span of time.

Despite being abused at home and at school, Shawn never complained. Rumors swirled for years that he trained to learn Karate from a neighbor and exacted his revenge on those same bullies years later. That was the one thing Jeff, and all the others could never understand or comprehend. Shawn was most likely the best hitter on the team, yet he was relegated to the bench because the rest of the team despised him.

How was that fair to a young teen who was considered miniscule in his own world? Jeff entertained the idea to be in Shawn's shoes, but he couldn't stomach the notion for a second. Slamming his fist on the steering wheel, visions of the past penetrated his mind and guilt began to set in. It took several years to worry about a teen that was once his friend. Jeff and the rest of the school took the young man into their lives and surrounded him with hate.

"How in the world could we get this so wrong?" Jeff shouted.

Jeff sat in disbelief with tears running from his eyes and began to delve deeper into a forgotten solace. The memories he was glad to retain were the first day he heard about a young kid on the freshman football and baseball teams that had recently thrown five touchdown passes and struck out nineteen batters in the same calendar year. Jeff was a sophomore at Masconomet High School and rumors were swirling about this young freshman with a gifted arm. It was the beginning of a curiosity for a boy that would eventually become a myth to himself and many others over the years to come.

Chapter 2
Stairway to Hell

The year is 1986 and my family and I have arrived in the small town of South Weymouth from the large state of Texas. The small two-story town home on Lyra Drive is part of a large community comprised of military families and base personnel. The South Weymouth Military base was the new destination of duty for Petty Officer Gary Wallis. My father was a part of the US Coast Guard and in his thirteen years of existence, I had found my sixth destination. Unable to maintain a decent childhood, the life of a military family exposed the loss of friends and misery for me and my sister, Mandy. The invitations of birthday parties and friendship were completely uninviting to both of us as we remained inside of our family's strict circle. Hidden deep into the realm of the Wallis family lay a shadow amongst our own circle of misery. Fractured and unwilling to speak, Mandy and I survived the agony of a severely abusive father and mother. Unable to escape physical beatings and sexual escapades, we would somehow remain far apart within only seconds of our miserable realities. The city of Weymouth was unprepared for the brutality of its own demise as a young man would venture into the hallways of its Junior High School in the late Summer of 1986. It was nothing close to the season of the witch, but if you stay with me here, you are going to understand the life of one person who would endure a life of pain and evil.

Confident and shy, I was a slim five-foot creature dressed in cheap clothes, worn tennis shoes and my hair looked like cat shit. I weighed barely over one hundred and thirty-five pounds, and the wind could blow me over if it wanted. In case I hadn't mentioned it, my parents were heavy smokers, and they preferred a carton of cigarettes over buying some decent fucking clothes for their son and daughter. I was in the middle of missing my friends back in the town of Hitchcock, Texas and as a product of a dysfunctional environment, I had no say in where we moved. Mandy didn't care either way because she was glad to have stayed away from our predator grandfather, Richard Wallis. I will spare you the gory details for now, but let's just say that our beloved father's dad poked and prodded Mandy like a pin cushion and he didn't give a shit. Despite her young age, Richard satisfied his psychotic appetite with predator-like reflexes and my sister had to bear it. Not until recently when our grandmother died, did my father show any emotion towards the relapses of judgement. She was Richard's wife, and her death exposed our family within its own dysfunctional circle. I barely shed a tear at her funeral and my father never forgave me for that over the years. I suffered a horrific beating over it, but I was used to it by then. After what I had known and the sexual perverse things grandpa did to Mandy, why would I cry or worry about another beating? Some part of me always knew that his clueless wife was behind his appetite, and I took that anger into my first day of Junior High.

The bus ride to school was smooth and quick, simply because it was barely a couple of miles away from home. Located just outside the fences surrounding the military base, there were bus stops for the students to wait and that is when I met a ridiculous number of teens my age. I always kept a wall up with new friends because I knew that I was going to have to pack up my shit and move again. I wasn't living a glorious life, but it was mine and I was trying to make the most of it. Upon entering the front doors of South Weymouth High School, the smell of newly waxed floors and old wood clogged the passages to my nostrils. It was the smell of excitement and despite my stupid appearance, I was attempting to learn everything I could. This is going to be a challenge because I was used to schooling in the southern states, but the first few hours I had arrived, I knew there lied an obstacle. The curriculum throughout the day in each class was harder and stricter. The teachers were all in their late forties and very confrontational with the students in each class. I was considered the new kid on the block, so I attempted to remain quiet for the first few months of school. While each day passed, I was beginning to fit in quite comfortably with everyone. I never really attempted to befriend anyone because I knew there was a chance my father was moving us to an actual home. I was tired of living in these townhomes' day after day and when it came time to apply for housing, our father informed the family of our chances. The list was long, but we all had faith in the system and Gary was trying.

Every day was repetitive, and it was a pair of eyes that caught my attention after months of boredom. Her name was Linda Lambiase and she was something else in my world of loneliness. She was in a few of my classes, and she had this baby face with beautiful red hair and cute lips. She wasn't gorgeous by any means, but she had this Wynona Judd thing going on and I was a huge fan of the country group, The Judds. She was endearing, sweet and when it came time to attend her classes, my heart melted. I was in a state of shock as my crush would soon capture my heart and I had to do something to entice my eyes. It was a cold night in December before Christmas when I worked up the courage to call her. This is 1986 people, and we didn't have the luxury of internet or google. I had to find this girl's number the old-fashioned way and patiently sift through the local phone book. With the assistance of my sister, she began dialing the number we had found under her last name. She was the only Lambiase in town and when the dial tone began, my heart sank into my stomach.

"Hello", the gentle voice mentioned.

Hesitating with fear, Mandy punched me in the arm and woke me up.

"Hi. Is this Linda?" I asked with nervousness.

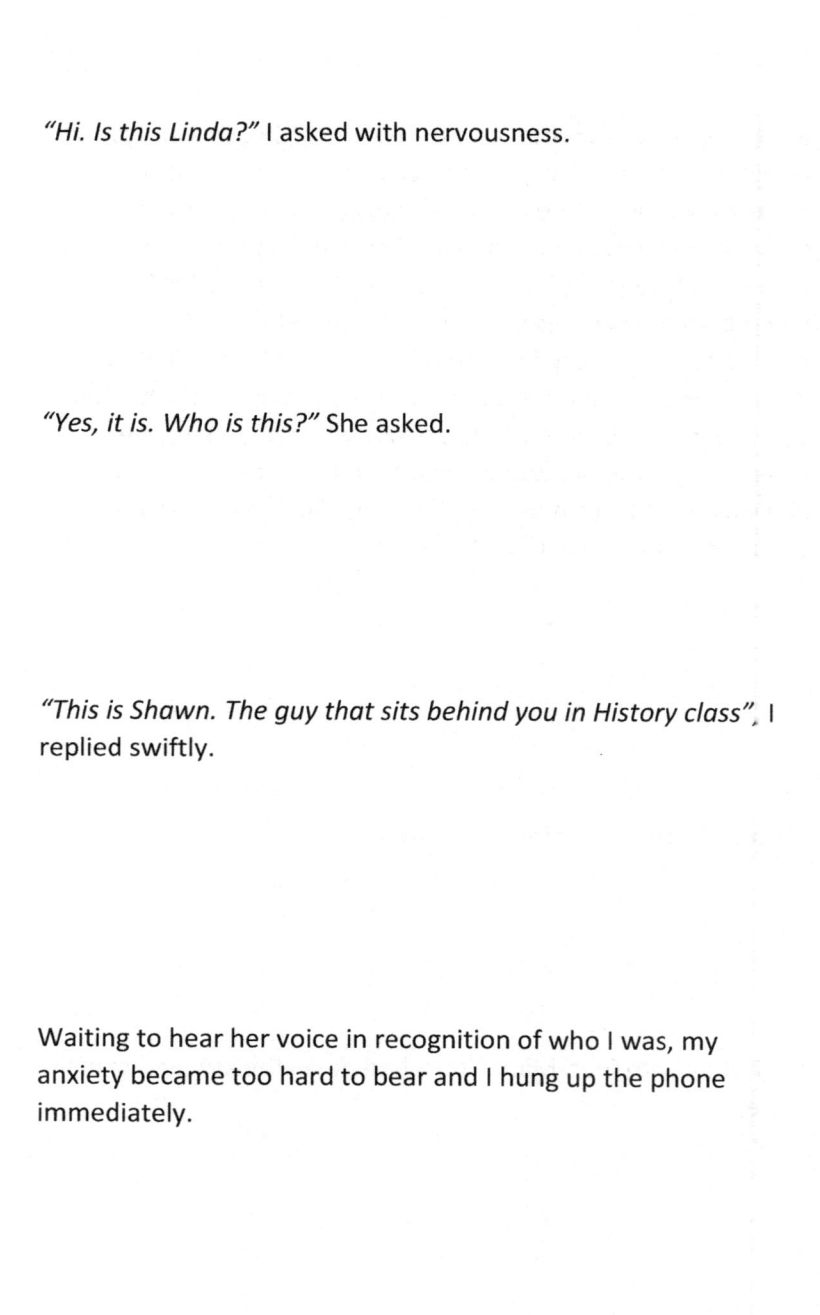

"Yes, it is. Who is this?" She asked.

"This is Shawn. The guy that sits behind you in History class", I replied swiftly.

Waiting to hear her voice in recognition of who I was, my anxiety became too hard to bear and I hung up the phone immediately.

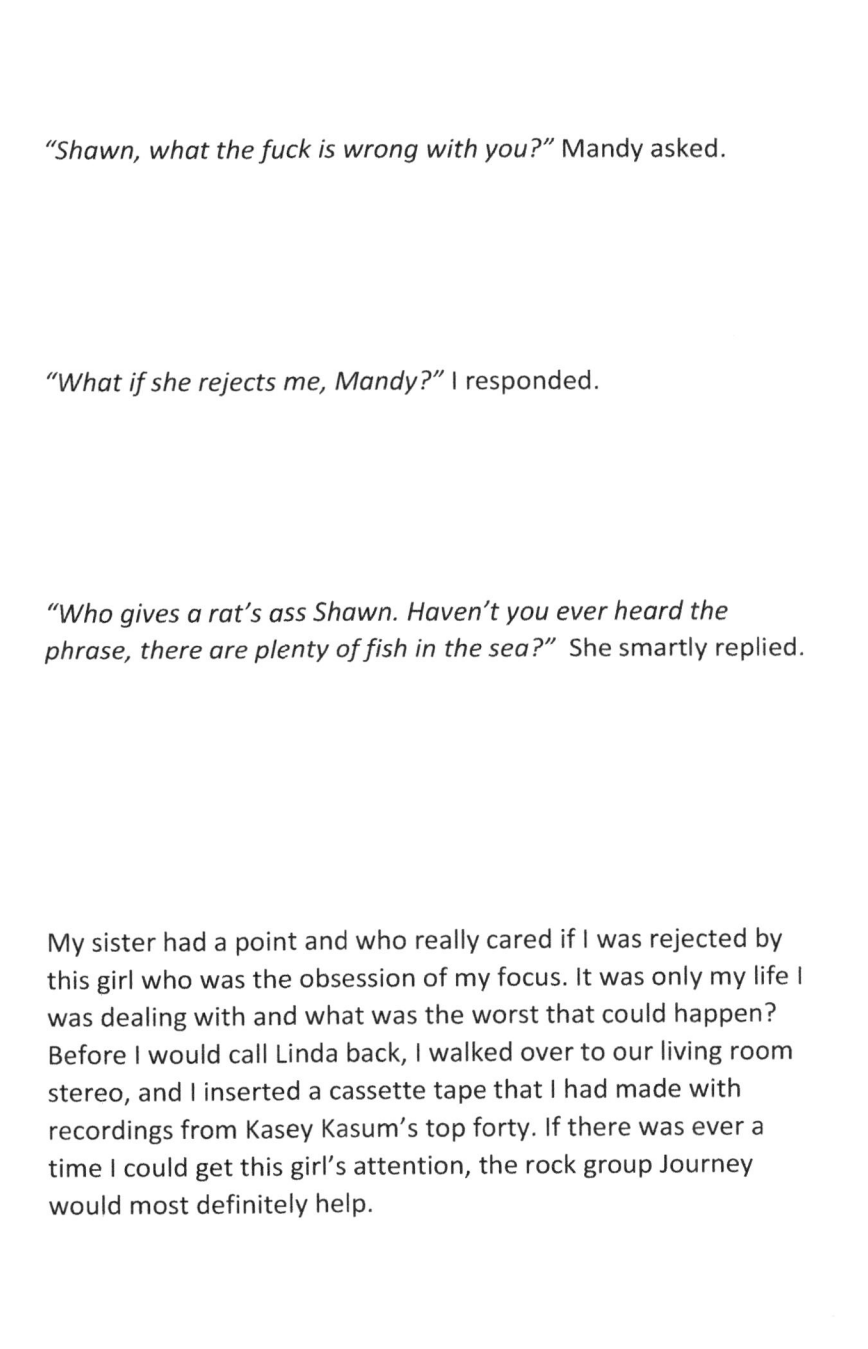

"Shawn, what the fuck is wrong with you?" Mandy asked.

"What if she rejects me, Mandy?" I responded.

"Who gives a rat's ass Shawn. Haven't you ever heard the phrase, there are plenty of fish in the sea?" She smartly replied.

My sister had a point and who really cared if I was rejected by this girl who was the obsession of my focus. It was only my life I was dealing with and what was the worst that could happen? Before I would call Linda back, I walked over to our living room stereo, and I inserted a cassette tape that I had made with recordings from Kasey Kasum's top forty. If there was ever a time I could get this girl's attention, the rock group Journey would most definitely help.

Upon dialing her phone number, I began playing the song, *"Don't Stop Believing"* in the background. The sound was low enough as the dial tone gave way to her beautiful voice, and she introduced herself once again.

"Linda, this is Shawn again. I am sorry I hung up the phone. Honestly, I am nervous, and I have never done this before", I replied.

"Is that Journey I hear in the background? That is my favorite song right now", she commented.

I wanted to be honest and just let my feelings flow through my voice and that was the first of many mistakes. What sense would it make to lie to this girl when I had to see her face in the morning?

"I chose this song for you, and I hoped you would really like it", I mentioned.

"I think it is sweet. You said your name is Shawn, right?" She asked.

"Yes. I am sorry I never spoke to you that much before", I replied.

"Yeah, me too. You have been sitting behind me all these months and all you do is stare at me", Linda exclaimed.

"It isn't you I am staring at. You just happen to be in front of the class and I have no other vantage point to see the chalk board", I smartly stated.

"Well said", my sister whispered in my ear.

Reluctant to say anything incorrect, I held my ground, bit my upper lip and spoke from the heart.

"Linda, I think you are quite beautiful. You remind me of a country singer I like, and I was wondering if we could talk more and get to know one another?" I asked with one eye open.

"Let me guess. Wynona?" She laughed out loud.

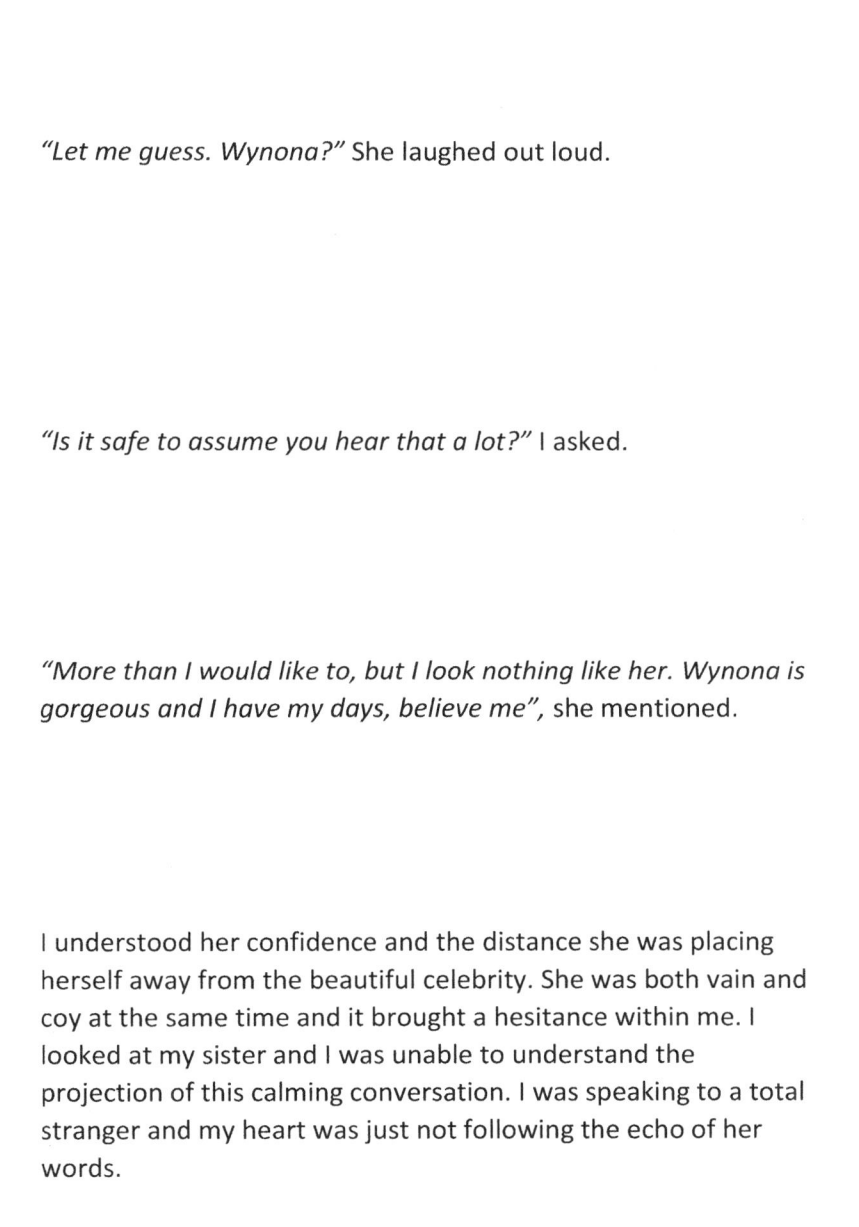

"Is it safe to assume you hear that a lot?" I asked.

"More than I would like to, but I look nothing like her. Wynona is gorgeous and I have my days, believe me", she mentioned.

I understood her confidence and the distance she was placing herself away from the beautiful celebrity. She was both vain and coy at the same time and it brought a hesitance within me. I looked at my sister and I was unable to understand the projection of this calming conversation. I was speaking to a total stranger and my heart was just not following the echo of her words.

"Linda, I think I am going to let you go. I appreciate you talking with me", I quickly stated before I hung up the phone.

The remainder of the night allowed me to lay my conscious mind upon the pillow and render my thoughts useless. I was introducing myself to an evil I had no idea was waiting for me and if I knew the conversation was going to start something horrible, I would have never called back. The phone call to Linda was a huge mistake and it became the focus the next morning in class.

"Good morning, Sunshine", the soft voice mentioned.

I turned around in my desk and Linda was staring over my shoulder looking down on me. For the first time, she glorified her face with makeup that Tammy Faye Baker would be jealous of. Her dollish face swallowed my eyes and with a quick whimper, I responded.

"Good morning. Are you mad at me?" I asked.

"Quite the opposite Shawn. I am glad you called me, and I wanted to chat with you for a minute before class starts", she stated.

It was a few minutes before class was beginning and with the hand of the clock staring at ten minutes after 7:00 am, the room slowly filled with students.

"I think you are a sweet guy and I want you to look over at Zack over there. Do you see how he has nice, feathered hair and he is wearing a nice shirt?" She mentioned.

I nodded towards Zack as he stared back at me with a gaze of excitement and a jerkish smile.

"I am attracted to boys like him, and I really don't like your curly hair. As a matter of fact, if I had money on me, I would take the time to get you a better shirt", she meanly replied.

Staring down at my blue shirt, Linda was right. My parents were horrible at getting me clothes and I had been an embarrassment for quite a few years. My mother was the primary shopper and she rather be at home smoking two cartons of cigarettes and watching the Price is Right. The parents I had were irresponsible and didn't care about the way my sister and I looked. Gary and Terri Wallis were prodigies of their addictions to nicotine and alcohol, and it affected their children.

"I am sorry you feel that way and thanks for letting me know something I already knew", I responded.

Linda Lambiase was a mean-spirited bitch and shame on her parents for raising a spoiled brat. She was correct in her critique of me because I looked like a prodigy of the 1970's. I wore a long-sleeved shirt with jeans and my hair was thick, bushy, and curly. Honestly, I looked as if I could have been a model for most elderly women wanting a perfect perm. I blame that shit on my dumb ass grandmother. A year before, my mother's mom decided to fuck with my hair, and it delighted them to a

defining moment of embarrassing their own blood. When I was growing up, I was labeled a cute kid with blonde hair and blue eyes. That all changed when I turned twelve and that innocent look disappeared quicker than I could blink. As you can see above here, the picture of me with Uncle Jim was horrific. Look at that afro! No wonder Linda was disgusted in me, and it was safe to assume other girls thought the same.

I wasn't expecting to hear her horrible rhetoric about my appearance, but it relaxed me a little. I lost interest the prior evening and I dedicated the rest of the year in motivating my brain to excel in my schoolwork. I contemplated asking the teacher to relocate my seat in the classroom, but it would favor my fear and decided to remain calm. Never in a million years would I have contemplated the phone call to Linda beginning a sequence of events changing my life forever. The wheels of motion began spinning and it was her current boyfriend that decided to interfere.

For unknown reasons, I was confronted with the whispers around school that this idiot teen wanted to fight me. Just for shits and giggles, let's label him with a name I consider suitable. His name is dick fuck and he looked like the type of guy Linda was attracted too. Apparently, the rumor swirling around school was his dislike of me flirting with his girlfriend. I was the basis for his hatred and with his friends surrounding him, he approached me in Math class one snowy afternoon.

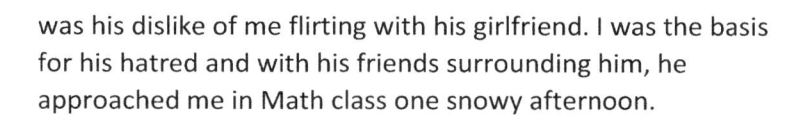

"Shawn Wallis. So, how would you like to meet after school today and duke it out?" Dick fuck asked.

Breathing with a deep sigh, I had no idea how to fight and without hesitation, I nodded my head yes in response to his desperation.

The idiot was a bit taller than me, but we appeared to weigh close to the same. There was no clear advantage for either teen, but I had a huge disadvantage in this upcoming match. His friends would outweigh the many invisible friends I had, and the setting would place us in the woods next to the school.

Weighing heavily on my mind during school was the fight against dick fuck and his miniscule appetite. Glaring at the clock on the cafeteria wall, I was mere hours away from the beating I deserved. I took the time to walk out of the front doors of the school and disappear into the basement below. It was a special placed I learned earlier in the school year, and it was my current salvation. I needed time to garner the strength to face the asshole who had no reason to fight me. Maybe I was different or maybe I was a tad bit unlucky when I made the phone call to Linda. Despite my feelings, I could care less, and I attempted to spend the next few hours delving into my mind. What was I possibly seeking you ask? Well, imagine being in my shoes here and doing whatever it took to recover motivation for this stupid fight? In my mind, the only way I had a chance was to ignite an anger deep within myself.

Spending nearly two hours in silence, my mind had wondered to the one place I feared the most. Growing up in the Wallis household was not an easy feat for anyone. It would take twenty plus years of my life to realize that Gary Wallis was not my real father, and it is a shame my parents lied to me all those years. The one thing that it does explain are the beatings I took my entire life. I needed motivation for this upcoming fight, so I began recollecting all the moments Gary Wallis took his aggressions out on me. He was a piece of shit drunk that would come home after work, drink himself to death and then find his way into my room. This occurred weekly for many years and to understand his reasons are the same as understanding a serial killer's motives.

Gary Wallis was a product of his own abusive environment. He was whipped and beaten by his father over the course of his childhood and somehow, he needed to pass that onto me. There was never any excuse for his abusive behavior, but to understand his logic defied all means to an end. The worst beating was a few years earlier in the small town of Hitchcock, Texas. A small rural area near the shores of Galveston, the afternoon was quite warm, and I had just come home from a venture into the woods. We lived in a beautiful neighborhood and our family lived in a three-bedroom house on the outskirts of town. I think it is safe to assume Gary was having a bad day and the smell of alcohol seeped through his pores.

"Shawn, where the fuck have you been?" He asked.

"Mom didn't tell you. I was with my friends in the woods", I explained with a nervous tone.

"Shawn, this is fucking 1984 and it doesn't take a rocket scientist to figure that you could be taken away from us. Don't you remember what happened to Adam Walsh a couple of years ago?", He asked with a yell.

Adam Walsh was the young boy taken from a Sears Department Store in the town of Hollywood, Florida back in 1981. We had been living in Key West at the time, so everyone was on h gh alert with their kids, and my father was no exception. The fear spread throughout Florida and to the killer hadn't been discovered until the year 2008.

"How many fucking times have I told you that your mother isn't the boss around here?" Gary stated.

Attempting to raise my hands to protect my face, Gary went on a rampage. He began swinging his fists left and right at my skull and pinned me against my bedroom wall. With no place to go, his brutal temper took its toll on me. When I finally placed my hands down, he reached down and pulled me up by my short hair. The pain was unbearable through my neck as he began to place his hands around my throat. Squeezing with all his might, my state of consciousness was loosely falling apart. I began to fade as he lifted me off the ground to kill me without hesitation. To this very day, I can't understand why my mother came in and stopped him. The moment of nearly dying in this psycho's hands, my mother became the focus of his anger. She reached behind him and grabbed her husband and began hitting him in the back of the head. Gary dropped me to the ground, and I was grasping for the little air that I had deserved. Looking up as my eyes were swollen shut, I could see my mother taking an extreme beating from her husband. This cowardly piece of shit was beating on a young teen and a woman, but never found the nerve to attempt a beating on another man. The rage in his eyes should have put him in jail, but my mother survived the attack and worked things out with the drunk piece of shit.

It was one of hundreds of beatings I took as a kid, and I could never understand why my mother never left him. I recall the separation between them in 1983 as my sister and I moved with my mother from Key West to Connecticut. It lasted only a few months and before we knew it, the asshole was back in the saddle and beating us once again.

Sitting next to the boiler in the basement, the warmth of the heat calmed my nerves as I recall my sister becoming the obsession of my grandfather. I had no idea that Gary's father was molesting her, and she never confided until she told my mother. It was the fear of losing the attention of my grandfather that kept things silent, but it was the unwanted attention of my uncle that scared the shit out of me. His name was Uncle Frank and his obsession with me was scary and cruel. He had a secret hatred for me because he was very close to my sister and as kids, we would celebrate our sibling rivalry with fighting. Uncle Frank couldn't put up with that and I recall his anger focused on my bare rear end. It was late one night in the early years of the 1980's and as a child, I made a habit of sleeping in my own bed at Uncle Frank's house. He lived in the beautiful post card town of Chester, Connecticut and my sister and I feared his home something fierce. Considered a pack rat, this vivacious home was full of antique furniture, tons of bedrooms and a hidden passage from the kitchen to an upstairs bedroom. The house was built like a fortress and there was a specific room that bothered our minds. It was the room at the south of the house that garnered our fears because a taxidermist worked their magic on several animals hanging on the walls. As a young boy, it was terrifying to stare at the head of a wolf wanting to snarl back at you. I swear there were times when that head wanted to take a snag at my sister and me. In relation to its compromise, I became obsessed with wolves later in life. I always pinpointed the beginning of my obsession to his house and that beautiful wolf on the wall. It spoke to me silently and began a world I wanted to be very much a part of.

It was a snowy evening one night when I realized I wasn't alone in my room. The room I stayed in was next to the secret passageway and I felt as if the strength of ten armies pinned me down. I was at the tender age of 10 when I felt the sharp pain inside my rectum that cold night. I was scared beyond recognition and the hand over my mouth silenced my screams. The gyration of his hips pushed further towards me, and he kept pulling away. With each thrust towards me, the pain became significant and his breathing against my ears became heavier. The smell of aftershave and old spice rummaged through my senses as he lay on top of my body. The grunting from this predator obviously became louder as he continued edging his way inside me. With my eyes buried in the pillow below me and his hands over my mouth, I experienced the brutal attack without having the chance to get away. This coward snuck into my body in the middle of the night and ravaged the innocence of his own nephew. The pain began to subside as he whispered in my ears.

"Leave your sister alone god damn you".

My rapist was never prosecuted and to this day, neither was my sister's. My sister and I were part of a family of crazy fuckers and Gary Wallis was just as abusive, if not worse. I was raped the one time by my uncle and that asshole died just last week. They found him on the floor of his own home, suffering a massive heart attack. How ironic his death was to become because his sister died the week before. Gary Wallis lost his mother and his uncle within a week; I considered their deaths a punishment well deserved. As I mentioned earlier, I failed to shed a tear for Gary's mother during her funeral. How am I supposed to mourn the death of a wife of a child molester? I knew she somehow was involved in both our rapes and to this day, I smile every time I think of their sudden passings.

God works his magic in mysterious ways and this book is the first time I have mentioned my rape and my accuser. There was no way I was going to take the time to worsen the beatings from Gary and his sadistic temper. My anger began building and I was a mere thirty minutes away from the clock striking 3pm. I spent hours in the basement reflecting on my past and I have never forgiven my rape and all the subsequent beatings that followed. What was this man's motivation to beat on a kid that wasn't his? Ever heard that line, *beaten like a red-headed stepchild.* I was living the meaning my entire life and I was becoming fearless. The beatings were brutal, but my body began understanding the bruises. During my years growing up, several teachers had seen bruising and markings on my body, but never took the time to call the police. See, the one thing Gary never understood was the ramifications of his behavior. If he had been arrested or convicted of the crimes against me, he could have lost his career with the Coast Guard. Honestly, I truly think he didn't care and as I would begin High School next year, the beatings and abuse didn't stop.

Psyched into oblivion, I felt enough anger to face this dick fuck of a person who thought he could bully his way through my time here in school. The beatings from my drunk father prepared me for this moment and as the school bell rang, I found myself outside in the cool air of the parking lot.

Chapter 3
The River of Darkness

Despite the bitter cold and the warmth of the bus, I neglected to bring a jacket to school. Never in my wildest dreams did I expect to have a fight today, but here I was. Dick fuck and his friends were waiting for me in the parking lot and as I arrived, I followed the collection of nosey students. A total of fifteen people were in attendance, and we all walked on the path through the soccer field next to the school. The chilling air froze the joints in my body, but the warmth of my anger kept me in check. Not one person was in my favor as this idiot collaborated his willingness to beat my ass. It was a rather peaceful walk to the opening of the woods. The sounds of chirping birds and the crackling of limbs in the wind muffled the silence in the air. My concentration was on Rocky Balboa and his fourth film. I had studied the film many times and I was prepared to offer a fight this dick fuck could never forget. I had the arm of a good pitcher in baseball and a jump shot like no other in Basketball. I think it was safe to assume I was a decent athlete, and I could find my way to fight decent.

As we approached the center of the woods, a campfire had already been started previously. The smoke enticed the woods and its clean air as the flame offered heat for the spectators. A few other boys had been waiting for our arrival and it was understood they were here for the fight. Speaking to an acquaintance named Jason Anderson, he informed me one of the boys waiting was dick fuck's older brother. Michael Tessier was another in attendance and he was subtle enough to help me with his guidance. All were unaware of the intentions of the awaiting boys, but it was understood that dick duck was an amateur when it came to fighting, and had no business being here.

The several square feet of open space offered the setting for our epic match, and I walked up without hesitation. My eyes focused on the opponent and his scrawny build. He seemed too relaxed for a fight, and it was my chance to silence him and his friends.

"I am ready if you are", I shouted.

"Wow, he seems ready I believe", as he laughed while looking at his friends.

Dick Fuck was unprepared for what was to happen, and he had no regards for his own safety. Attempting to throw a punch in my direction, I ducked with ease. It was Rocky part three in my mind and Clubber Lang was overconfident and swinging like a mad man without landing one punch. This was no different and I sat back and watched this idiot wear himself out in the first few seconds of this fight. Tired and nearly worn down, I faked a jab from my left and upon him turning his head away, I nailed him hard with a right. The strength of the landing knocked dick fuck backwards and on his ass. I couldn't believe the power I had displayed, and I felt as if I was stronger. The shouting of his friends for him to get up and continue broke the silence of the woods. Standing in the cold air and waiting for him to get back on his feet, I patiently approached with my hand extended. It was a move I will regret, but I offered to help him back up.

The small window of kindness backfired, and dick fuck grabbed my hand and kicked me in the groin from his crouching position. Lucky for me the shot landed on my inner thigh, and I was slowly stunned enough to back up and give my opponent time to get on his feet. Stepping forward, I noticed a boy behind me getting closer. It took a mere second to realize I was in trouble and within a second, I lunged forward and landed a left uppercut on the jaw of the man standing in front of me. Knocking dick fuck to the ground was the beginning of the end for the fight, but something was wrong. Looking down on the teen I had merely knocked out, the shouting of a loud voice silenced my win.

"Get him", a loud voice shouted.

I was grabbed from behind and thrown to the ground as I looked up into the breaking of the trees. The bluish skies were my focus as punch after punch landed on my face and split my head wide open. The silhouette of five boys began kicking punching and bludgeoning my body with anger over their friend's ass whooping. Pinned to the ground, I began closing my eyes and imagined my beatings over the years while covering my face. The pain throughout my body subsided and all I could feel was the weightlessness of my own mind. The sound of stomping and punches grew silent as my world became smaller.

The feeling of branches and sticks compiling bruises upon my body hurt the most. Comfortably numb, my imagination drifted away and temporarily brought my soul away from the beating. I can look down with ease and see the silhouette of several boys surrounding my torn body. I wanted so badly to get up and whoop their asses, but my guilt struck my thoughts down with a whimper. Echoes of anger rushed through the silence of the woods, as the beating lasted a mere sixty to ninety seconds. I was left lying on the ground with my face in shambles, broken bones throughout my body, and a blood-soaked shirt. It was a wonder how I didn't piss myself through the chaos, but I turned over helplessly and took a deep breath.

Facing down into the frozen ground, I placed my hands under my chest, and I calmly forged my legs to follow suit. I was determined to get up and see this through and show all these cowards I was not afraid. As my body began rising, I looked to my right and saw the few boys that were responsible for this cowardly beating. Staring back up into their faces brought a memory I most likely would be living with forever. The look of disgust and worry covered their expressions as my blood-shot eyes scared the life out of them. Some of the bullies attempted to cover their faces knowing I was someday going to seek revenge, if any at all. All the teens witnessing my beating began to understand my strength as I slowly placed my legs beneath my body. It was a metamorphosis in the making and each set of eyes were astounded by what they were seeing. My face was swollen, and my eyes could barely puncture my abated skin. The look from the strangers in the woods plundered my silence and I could hear them cheer me on.

"Get up Shawn, you can do it", a voice in the background said aloud.

Inching closer to my destiny, I used the remaining strength within my lower body to slowly stand. My body was weak and cosmetically torn, but my legs were my strength. It took five courageous boys to tear me down, but it was going to take a complete army to keep me from getting up. The chilling wind soothed my oxygen as the blood in my eyes prevented my vision to remain clear. Looking to my left, the remaining teens bear witness to a miracle never seen before. The young man with his broken jaw, torn face, broken nose, ripped and bloody clothes, broken ribs, his jarred spirit and bloody crystal blue eyes defied all odds. This hero took a humongous beating and stood in front of them without one complaint. His faint lips, cracked and bruised, began opening for their ears to listen

"Is this what you all came for? Did you think for one second that someone like me deserved this? I didn't ask to be here and sure as hell didn't think this would be how my day ended. I want you all to look at me one good time and see that you did not defeat me. I promise you that I will seek those responsible and I swear to you that I will be back", I stated with a broken murmur and tears running down my face.

Standing with confidence, I began to slowly walk towards the path of the river. It was bright red and the blood in my eyes had shaded the beauty of Earth's most pleasant attribute. I had no ride home, there was no bus waiting for me, and since the trip was brief, I walked home next to the body of water. What other choice did I have really? I was hell bent on getting to the one place I could rest easier. I was slowly fading, and the insides of my body were falling apart with each step in the cold. The temperature of the air quickly dropped as the minutes passed. It was nearing night fall and the slush under my feet soaked my shoes and numbed my toes. The noticeable limp prevented my quick departure home, but this heart was beating steady. I followed my soul as far as a I could and within hours, I was nearing the front entrance of the South Weymouth military base. The entire walk from the Junior High seemed like an eternity, but I would not succumb to my injuries. Barely able to stand, I arrived at the front gate disabled and weak. I kneeled to the pavement and literally fell to the awaiting arms of the guard on duty.

He was able to collect a little information to contact my parents. It was the call I wish hadn't happened, but within a few minutes, my mother collected herself and picked me up. Frantic tears streamed from her face while she quickly ran me to the hospital. Without hesitation, my mother for once became someone I needed. Despite all the beatings I had taken my entire life, she understood the priority of my well-being. Her son was slowly fading, and it was on her conscience to save me. It was nice to finally see that someone gave a shit about me in this family. The Sargent at the front gate notified the authorities of my beating and were aware of my arrival at the South Weymouth Hospital. Once I had penetrated the sliding glass doors of the Emergency Room, the entire staff took notice. My appearance seemed like I had a huge fistfight with Freddy Kreuger and my heartbeat was slowly fading.

Unaware of my collapsed lung, the stress of my injuries pressured my heart to immediately stop as I fell to the floor. I was dying and five boys were responsible for my death, and they would more than likely spend the rest of their lives in prison. Lying on the floor, I suddenly woke up and stood to my feet in mere seconds. Upon rising, I felt surrounded by a warmth I couldn't explain. The lights around me were bright and I was greeted by several children. Mixed in ages from three to five years old, they delightfully grabbed my hands and lead me down the hallway. Their joy uplifted me and when we arrived at the end of the hall, I looked upon a boy who was covered in wires to his body. Looking closer, it appeared I was laying on a bed surrounded by nurses.

There was a young girl holding my hand and she looked up at me while squeezing my fingers. She was attempting to covet my fear with her beautiful blue eyes, but she suddenly spoke.

"Shawn, it is going to be alright. It isn't your time yet. I want you to come with me because I want you to meet someone", she whispered with a giggle.

Looking down at my bruised and battered body, a tear relinquished itself from the corner of my eye. The stream of salt slid down my face and onto the palm of the young girl. She let go of my hand and instantly cupped her hands together. The tear she delightfully caught turned from a small spec of water into a white light. Within seconds, the light became brighter as a small circle appeared, hovering above her open hands. The scene was something out of a movie and I was astounded of its beauty.

"Look closer Shawn. Look into your destiny", the soft voice stated.

I bent on one knee and focused closer on the small globe above her hands. The mystic sphere began to show signs of an environment with teenagers dressed in baseball and football uniforms. The colors were red and white, and the helmets and hats had the letter M stitched on them. They appeared to be standing together and pointing fingers at something facing my direction. Standing on what appeared to be grass, the look in their faces was mystic. It was a feeling in my gut as if they were looking for someone to lead them.

"What are they pointing at?" I calmly asked.

"Why don't you ask them?" She replied with a giggle.

I looked down upon them as if I was Gulliver and simply asked the one question that came to mind.

"What are you pointing at may I ask?"

If this were a movie, I think we all would anticipate the small voice of an angel echoing from a distance. I was expecting something that was never going to happen, and it was a blessing because I kept my sanity. Staring into the small eyes of each person in the globe, I recall a dream I once had years ago. I was living in a small house and for some strange reason, I was followed by one person and then two. It would continue for hours as if an entire army would follow me and stop when I ceased walking. I found it to be terrifying, but the Deja vu moment was coming to me and it explained a lot. Maybe I was imagining an interstellar moment or some eclipse of life flashing before my eyes. Before I could conjure up another thought, my small angel began speaking.

"Shawn my dear. You are staring at your future. It is a bright and lonely world looking for a special purpose. I am truly sorry for what has happened to you here, and we are giving you a second chance", **the young girl stated.**

"A second chance? I never knew I had a first chance. Are you saying that I died?" **I asked with purpose.**

"Death is beautiful, isn't it? Shawn, you have been closely followed your whole life and you have suffered greatly at the hands of the man you call your father", she calmly replied.

"I am used to the beatings over the years, but I just can't understand why he hates me so much", I replied.

"He is not your father Shawn. The man that attempts to care for you is someone that was placed in your world of adversity", she truthfully stated.

"What the fuck? Are you telling me the truth here? He is not my father?" I asked as I could barely breath.

"Relax Shawn. Think closely. Go back into your life and look at all the coincidences and add them up. We have always kept an eye on you and helped when the time was right. Do you recall the night before you went to school today? Do you remember the dream with the angel?" She asked.

"Oh my god. That was you?" I shouted.

Closing my eyes, I could see her from my dream, and she was exactly how I remember her.

"I have always been here for you Shawn and I will continue to help as God permits", she stated.

"When you wake up, you are going to feel different. I am giving you a reason to be the leader you have always been. Don't take what you are getting for granted", she joked.

I couldn't believe I was in this miraculous dream and parts of my body felt as if they were tingling. Looking at the beautiful wings of the girl near me, I suddenly fainted. It was as if I fell asleep and when I closed my eyes, I began to drift back into reality. My body went from weightlessness to a sharp feeling of pain in my ribs. The sound of a constant beep coddled my ears, and the touch of a gentle hand soothed my fears. My heart was beating irregularly, and the coldness of the sheets kept me in a cocoon of safety. I gently opened my eyes and the brightness of the lights on the ceiling shaded my sight. The temperature was freezing, and the chattering of my teeth numbed my brain. I had woken up inside of a hospital room and the only soul in front of me was a beautiful young nurse.

"Good morning, Shawn, I am Breanna, and I will be your nurse today. Did you enjoy your three-day nap?" She asked.

Unable to say a word with tubes in my throat, I could barely envision the beauty of the woman near me. My eyes appeared hazy as everything appeared blurry. I felt helpless and alone and I wanted to go back to sleep and visit my angel once more. My parents and sister were nowhere to be found and the anger inside of my heart wanted to punch the man who called himself Dad. I couldn't believe he was an imposter all these years, but it began to make perfect sense. He prepared me for the vicious beating I suffered and all the years he threatened me. I was the red-headed stepchild in his mind, and I could only imagine what he really thought of me. Life was seeming unfair, and I was living in a nightmare all these years under the false pretense that I was surrounded by love. My mother could care less about what her husband was doing to me. I lay here bruised and battered while these assholes are at home wishing I would perish without a second thought. My angel had given me another purpose in life and just before I could endure more grief, the nurse arrived with a few of the staff. My focus was coming back, and I could see clear from my eyes of regret.

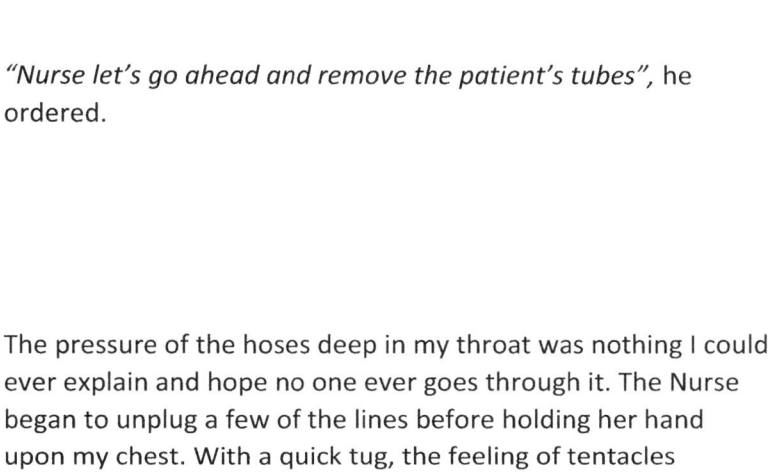

"Nurse let's go ahead and remove the patient's tubes", he ordered.

The pressure of the hoses deep in my throat was nothing I could ever explain and hope no one ever goes through it. The Nurse began to unplug a few of the lines before holding her hand upon my chest. With a quick tug, the feeling of tentacles escaping my gullet felt amazing. It was like I could breathe easier and with a swift motion, the hoses and tubes were away from my face.

"Hi Shawn. I am Doctor Reid, and you gave us a few scares over the last few days. How are you feeling? He asked.

Opening my mouth, the dry air sharpened my teeth with a feeling of pain in my jaw. I felt my swollen cheeks struggle to massage my lips as I tried to speak.

"Doc, what happened to me? Why am I here?" I stupidly asked.

"Shawn, you were severely beaten by several teens from your school. The Police have been here a few times and they told us your story", he kindly offered.

"How would they know unless I told them, which I don't think I did", I asked.

"A few witnesses came forward and told them the story and I need you to understand it's a miracle you are even alive. You flatlined on us a few times and somehow, you kept coming back", the Nurse replied.

"Where is my family?" I asked.

"We called them a short time ago when you woke up and they are on the way to see you", she replied.

"Shawn, you have broken ribs, a broken orbital bone surrounding your right eye. You suffered deep lacerations on your stomach and one of your kneecaps was broken. You have a punctured lung and your heart stopped twice. You are lucky to be alive Shawn", the Doctor stated while reading his chart.

I rolled my eyes as he was talking, and I clearly don't remember a fucking word he said. I wanted to immediately get up, walk out of this hospital and find the teens responsible for my near murder. I understood I had a new destiny to follow, but I was never told I couldn't exact revenge on the cowards that jumped me. I was in a clear state of anger and before I could think of a plan, I had to heal and get better. If I was going to spend a few days in the hospital, I could begin understanding the reasons for my appearance. Why in the world would a group of teens beat someone to near death? It was a question I had to penetrate, and I let the moment calm my fears.

In the few days I had rested in the hospital, the small miracle I had created was now coming to fruition. Something magical was happening and I became one of the most interesting cases in Massachusetts history.

"Doctor, Doctor", the nurse yelled.

"The X-Rays you had me take from our patient. Something is very wrong here", she shouted.

I was laying there on the bed feeling much better and listening to the drama unfold. The Doctor and Nurses were all failing to understand why my X-rays from a few days before and now were not matching. It was as if a magic wand had found its way into the hospital and healed my body.

"Something isn't right here. Are we sure this is the same patient", the Doctor replied.

The Doctor hadn't seen me since early yesterday and when he began checking my vitals and my eyes, a rapid change was discovered.

"This can't be. How in the world can you already be healed?" He nervously asked aloud.

I shook my head as if I had no idea what the hell he was talking about. I was not a miracle in anyone's eyes because I was just a thirteen-year-old little puke who got his ass kicked by a bunch of punks. I wasn't any different than the next kid, but I must agree that I was feeling much better. My vision came back clear, my head was no longer hurting, and my jaw felt perfect. While the dumb ass Doctor was ranting on, I removed the sheets from my body and noticed the bruises had disappeared. I noticed something else that is embarrassing to admit, but I think my Johnson grew a little. Nah, just kidding, but I made you think about it, didn't I?

I felt stronger and without hesitation, I sat up and began to place my legs over the gurney. With the Doctor and Nurse arguing over nothing, I found myself standing beside my bed.

"Is this good enough for you?" I asked aloud.

Holding his hands over his mouth, the clipboard dropped to the floor. Every one of the staff on this floor was now inside my room and nobody could believe what they were seeing. I was considered a miracle and I wanted to leave.

"Son! Oh my god, you are ok", my mother shouted as she ran inside the room to hug me.

"Mom, I am ok. Can you please take me home?" I asked.

Looking at the hospital staff, my mother told them I was coming home, and she was fearless. Nothing was going to take her words away from her and without hesitation, I was on my way. The exit from the hospital was overdue and there was only one thing on my mind. Revenge, revenge and more revenge on the kids who allowed themselves the opportunity to ruin my life.

I was met at home by the police chief of South Weymouth, and he had placed each teen in jail and then into custody of their parents. It was a vicious cycle and because I had miraculously recovered, I was asked if I wanted to press charges.

"Chief, I would like those boys to live their lives fearing what is behind them. Please allow them to go back to school and let fate decide their future", I commented.

Without a word, the man in uniform walked out of my front door to never be seen or heard of again. It was the words from my so-called father that placed me onto the beginning of a new direction.

"Son, I have great news. As of tomorrow, we are packing up and moving to Topsfield. I really didn't expect this for quite some time, but somehow, it's a miracle that you are here with us. I

didn't think two miracles would happen, but it has. You don't have to go to that stupid school anymore and we will enroll you as soon as we move", he spitted out.

The angel was right, and I couldn't take my mind off her. She was now placing my life into a new destiny, and I tried fighting my anger. I wanted to stay long enough to make those boys pay for what they did to me. If it was meant to be, I was going to find a way to visit these idiots when I could make the time.

"Dad, where is Topsfield", I asked with a small hesitation.

"It's north of Boston and almost an hour from here. We have been approved to move into a real house Shawn. I was also able to get you enrolled into summer baseball. Aren't you excited?" He asked me.

I honestly didn't give a shit what came out of his mouth anymore and my respect for him was gone many years ago. Gary Wallis was a child abusing, drunk asshole who took his aggressions on the one kid he resented the most. If I was going to survive from now on, I was going to do whatever it took to avoid him. As for baseball, I wasn't overly excited. I had a decent arm and a decent bat, so the idea that I was going to start every day was never going to happen. I was just another teen going through puberty and I needed to change a bit. If I was leaving South Weymouth to lead a better existence, I needed to change my appearance. I was tired of looking like a white teen with a huge afro and mustache. I was going to make things better for myself and it all started in the bathroom.

I walked upstairs into the town house and locked the bathroom door behind me. Equipped with a pair of scissors, trimmers and a razor, my life was about to become something better. I was bound for a new town, a new home, a new school and a better life. The mirror was staring back into my eyes and with each cut of my hair, I saw something magnificent. It was a teen slowly become more responsible and if I was to become a leader soon, I need to look the part. After an hour, I would answer my own question with a subpoena of thoughts rattling my mind. I removed my shirt and noticed something I hadn't before. The body was in more shape than ever before, and I literally had abs. I was defined as if I was exercising every day for the last year, and this was no joke. I was in shape, and I felt stronger than I ever have and with a new look in the mirror, I was now prepared to face a new horizon. The school was called Masconomet Regional High School and with only thirty days left in the school year of 1987, I enrolled. The front doors were synonymous to my purpose like a cloud of smoke before the fire. This town of Topsfield had never seen anything like my existence and without pause, I gently penetrated the student body with ease. It was my time to shine and without hesitation, I would spend the next thirty days accessing my surroundings and its purpose. It was the summer of 1987 that would clearly define my reason for living and it was an explosive debut.

Chapter 4
Next to Nothing

My debut in the first month of Junior High was nothing to write home about, but I survived. Why my parents chose to put me in school for only thirty days was one of life's mysteries, but it did offer me an idea of who my classmates were. I didn't spend a lot of time making friends since I was still placing a huge wall up around me. I trusted no one after the huge debacle at South Weymouth Junior High, so I relaxed and observed. It was a necessary evil to blatantly understand who I was going to befriend and avoid. My first day was easy and a young teen by the name of Cheryl Walton introduced herself. She was a bit different in that she dressed up in clothes resembling the Heavy Metal era. We are in the late eighty's people, so put your mind back at ease here. It was her wild hair, dark makeup, tight jeans and Metallica T-shirt that gave her away. It wasn't my ideal person to befriend, but she was the first to extend an olive branch. It was Cheryl that took the time to introduce me to her friends, and boy there were a lot of them.

I had slowly begun to realize the class I ventured into was split into several cliques. Just like any school, it was up to the new student to choose which side to integrate with. With the help of my new guide Cheryl, she took it upon herself on the first day to bring me on a tour at lunch. The cafeteria was shared by the large High School, and it was the first time I had seen a Junior High and High School integrate. Despite my shortcomings, I was focused on learning about this potential class in my future.

"Shawn, this is our cafeteria and as you can see, there are several circular tables that everyone is accustomed to sitting at", Cheryl mentioned.

Following her guide and her tight pair of jeans, she introduced me to each table in the cafeteria. Masconomet was comprised of several groups of people and this day was a learning lesson for sure. I was introduced to the jocks, the sluts, the metal heads, the smokers, the glamour girls, the nerds, the teachers' pets, the special needs, and most of all, the empty table.

The tour didn't last long, and I was not interested in most of the student body. I was unaware of their feelings for the new student at the time, so I chose to hang out with Chery's friends. They were comprised of drug addicts, smokers, tons of hair, and lots of makeup. I was not comfortable around these people, but

Cheryl took a huge liking to me, and it made being around her easier. I would refrain from telling her the truth about how I felt towards her friends.

Thanks to Cheryl and her gargoyle looking friends, I was able to waste a quick month of worthless classes and the summer began.

My father had us move to a small community called *The Nike Site*. It was located just outside the town of Topsfield on top of a hill off route one. It was a long highway stretching from Florida through Maine. We just happened to be living in a small neighborhood that was built back in the late sixties. The purpose of the houses was to allow the military to shelter their families while they worked on the adjacent nuclear base.

I said that right people! A nuclear base on the outskirts of Topsfield. When the Cuban missile crisis began in the early sixties, John Kennedy aligned the entire eastern seaboard with nuclear capabilities. Often called Nike Sites, the silos would become placed on standby in case of a nuclear war with Russia. Due to a huge false alarm, the base was closed and decommissioned in 1974. Unable to convince the government to shut the housing down, the military drowned the existing silos and condemned the remaining buildings. Separated by a large gate, the sixteen homes outside of the base were primarily used for current military personnel and their families. This began in the late seventies and my parents were a part of the project.

House number fifteen was located on top of the large hill of the Nike Site. When you drive off the highway and into the neighborhood, the homes surround a large hill and part of the community is on flat ground. The home was small, and our yard was a massive part of the corner of the street. On the opposite side of the road were three homes that faced our yard. It was a unique design since all sixteen homes were placed near the street.

Our home was tiny and consisted of three bedrooms. It wasn't glorious, but it was much better than the townhomes we had lived in before. Being a part of a military family had its ups and downs, but mostly downs if you ask me.

Unaware of the amount of rich people in this town, I had to make the best of what we could since we considered poor. My mother took it upon herself to sign me up for summer baseball. In the town of Topsfield, the Babe Ruth league was for kids from age 13-17. It was mighty quick to become part of a team I had known nothing about, but my arm felt good, and I took a few swings in the yard with my dad. If there was one thing, I could say about Gary Wallis that I enjoyed, it was his commitment to help me excel in baseball.

Growing up, I was always a part of some little league team, and I was never the best hitter or pitcher, but my father was dedicated. He wanted me to become better and all the nights of catching my fast balls and concentrating on my hitting were about to pay off in a huge way. I don't mind saying this, but to this very day, the old man thinks he was responsible for what you are about to read. I never allowed him to comprehend the true meaning behind my abilities, but why not dangle that piece of fruit. He was the most abusive man I have ever known and his control over me frightened my entire childhood. I was scared he would kill me at any moment, so I kept to myself from the ages of thirteen and on. I found every chance I could in hopes he would be on duty out on the ocean. Those were the times he would be gone for three and four months at a time and my life was soothing and easy. When it came time for him to be home, his obsessive drinking and visits to my room were an abundance of pain. I was beaten to a point of being scared to come out of my room, but the control Gary Wallis needed was only over me. He never attempted his psychotic behavior on my mother or my sister.

The summer of 1987 was in full swing, and I became a part of a try out located in the center of Topsfield at Proctor Field. When my mother drove me to the baseball field, I was elated at the number of teenagers trying out for the team. Apparently, the team was in existence for many years and had never been a part of a winning program. It was my time to shine, and I was introduced to a few teens I had recognized in school. Richard Crosson and Andrew Foreman were best friends, and they were part of the clique I remained far from. They were smart kids that came from wealthy parents, and I was looking for an affiliation to be respected by them and many others.

After an hour of the coach talking and directing, I came to the realization that Andrew Foreman was a second baseman and the son of the coach. Coach Foreman was a tall presence with brown wavy hair and a mustache only a mother could love. He was identifying the talent surrounding him on the ball field for the previous ninety minutes and it was my name he chose to call.

"*Shawn Wallis. Grab a bat son and let's see what you got*", he shouted.

Here I was, this fourteen-year-old kid with the weight of anxiety on his shoulders. I was built solid with bright blue eyes and the sweatpants I had chosen to wear, kept falling loosely from my waste. Standing in the batter's box, I looked towards coach and his delivery was smooth and inviting. With the quick swing of my thirty-two-ounce bat, I connected fluidly with the oncoming baseball. The sound of the horsehide and yarn swiftly echoed throughout the town as the ball landed into the tall grass in left field. Considered a homerun, the attention began to focus on me and no one else.

"Wow. Let's try that one again. Beginner's luck", Coach Foreman wittingly joked.

The eyes of everyone behind Homeplate and near the bench became fixated on my stance. The ball exited coach's hand and within a mere few seconds, the ball again left the field in a matter of moments. The second hit was further, and I was astounded at the new power I had found. My swing was fluent and easy, and it never changed over the many years in Little League.

"Son, where are you from?" Coach asked.

"I just moved here from south of Boston coach", I replied.

"I have never seen anything like this kid", Coach told his assistant.

With only a few more swings of the bat, I had collected a few homeruns and one wicked foul ball, nearly separating a bird from its body. The awe of every player on the baseball field congratulated me and without hesitation, I was the talk of the day. All the participants were greeting themselves and I felt as if I found something to where I belonged. Despite my introduction, the team was short of a pitcher and there were rumblings on the field. Ryan Guilbault had been the pitcher for the team in recent years, but he was not built for long games. Watching Ryan pitch in warmups on the first day, I was not impressed. He was fluid in his motion, but the ball came out too slow. Staring at his delivery from behind, I could see his hesitation and it was a major weakness.

He had a great curveball, but he tended to tip his pitches. As a batter, I would be licking my chops if this kid was on the bump in front of me. Since we were on the same team, it was time to put my critiques aside and handle the baseball. Coach asked everyone if they were interested in pitching, but in my eyes, it was a cry for help. Coach Foreman was looking for the missing piece and he found one of his best hitters in a matter of seconds. It was time for him to begin believing, as he witnessed my first pitch across home plate.

Standing on the rubber mound, I was considered an average pitcher over the years. I first found the mound at the tender age of seven in Key West, Florida. I was signed up for little league and my father thought I would be a delight on the mound. It was a miserable year as I surrendered more homeruns than the bat boy at a Boston Red Sox practice. I was awful and it was a huge let down. What my father did was ingenious, and he asked me to deal with massive diversity. I was starting to fail but isn't that a good idea when you have everywhere else to look up. I was on the bottom after the first year in little league and ever since then, my ability to become uncanny worked. I would successfully lead my next three teams to the playoffs.

Life becomes easier when you develop a few pitches in your arsenal. I felt as if that undefeated team in 1983 could have been the best Little League team in the country. I was three years into my career as a pitcher and a batter, and I was considered the best player in the league. I had worked hard for what I was earning and then my father announced we were moving to Texas.

Despite the massive move, my baseball career maintained itself in the small town of Hitchcock, Texas. For the first time in my life, I was now surrounded by kids of Spanish descent. Let me be honest with you about all of that. These kids were good, they were fast, and they could hit. I learned a lot in my couple of years in the town of Hitchcock and I took my newfound art of pitching to a whole new level. I developed an amazing curveball, change up, and fastball, and brought it to this moment on the mound.

Standing sixty feet and six inches away, I looked down the tunnel towards the catcher behind the plate. The twenty yards felt like an eternity, but the delivery of my first fastball pooped the catcher's mitt with a delightful echo. Regardless of its speed and protectory, the stiches of the baseball garnered the corner of the plate. The delivered strike was of many to come while the coaches, players and their parents watched in amazement. I was delivering persistent strikes in a fashion never seen from the arm of a teenager in their eyes.

My skin was riddled with goosebumps as each pitch became faster and faster. The palm of the catcher needed a break, and the coaching staff now had an ace to face the competition of their Babe Ruth League. Word was traveling fast in the tri-town areas of Middleton and Boxford, that Topsfield was a major contender for the summer.

Happy to be home and elated over making the team, my father and mother were arguing again. It was always something with these two unhappy people, and I just wish they would finally divorce. My mother was proud of my accomplishment, but my father didn't care. His drunk rage was on display again as the kitchen again would bear witness to his broken dishes. I couldn't count the number of times I would hear them argue over the many years, but my door remained lock and safe from the man who privately wanted to end my life. Gary was sulking in his booze and reruns of Happy Days and Laverne and Shirley. It wouldn't be long before he would pass out and maybe never wake up, but wishful thinking, right?

I was elated to be a part of a team that was the talk of the town and that was just on my first day. In the next week, we would hold several practices to project the positions for each player. When I wasn't pitching, I was relegated to playing Left Field. We already had a first baseman in Mike Lindquist, a catcher in Mike Panutich, a shortstop in Richie Crosson and of course, the team brat was playing second base. He was the coach's kid, and he would annoy me for years to come.

We had Scott Demers at third and his little brother Shaun in the outfield with Ryan Guilbault and I rounding out the roster. There was also Wade Twitchell and Dom Lomano among a few others helping the team. We had a great lineup, and our first game was against Boxford on a Wednesday evening. Of all times to have a game, let's go ahead and try the middle of the week. I wasn't speculating the stupidity of our schedule, but the breezy evening in the middle of late June was a perfect setting for a night of baseball. Boxford was a large town just west of Topsfield and since the game was a home game for us, we tempered their arrival. I was scheduled to pitch the seven-inning affair in my debut and bat in the third position for the game. When all was said and done, I had begun the first inning and ended the game with a strikeout.

In total, I would strike out sixteen Boxford batters and surrender one hit. Our team gracefully jumped all over Travis Larabee and his beautiful curveball. I had never seen a pitcher develop a curveball as a main pitch, but he was tricky at times during the first few innings. Upon surrendering several runs, he was relieved for someone else, and they didn't stand a chance. The fourteen to zero score reflected our team and its willingness to shadow a coach that wanted to excel in the league. I ended the game with five hits, three stolen bases and a dominant performance that echoed itself within the league.

Topsfield was a team to be reckoned with and the summer of 1987 began with a positive experience. We were next to nothing and teams within the league were developing fear as they played us. We began the season with four wins, and it was the existence of a Middleton team and its dominant pitcher that was gunning for our pride. This was the showdown that many would talk about before and after for years to come. Rick Anthony and his teammates were not afraid, and it was an epic game on their home turf. Whoever took this game was going to be in first place and had bragging rights in our league.

On a hot night in July, I arrived with my parents to the small ball field located in the center part of Middleton called Rubchinuk Town Park. It reminded me of the old days in Galveston, Texas with the small field, small grandstands and huge left field. Upon arriving in my Topsfield uniform, I was greeted with familiarity. People I had never met before began greeting me as if they knew who I was. This was a huge surprise to my parents and for the first time in their life, they had a son who was nearly a celebrity. The scents of the evening smelled of confidence and it was my first chance to tear apart the team that was favored to win our league. When everyone finally showed up and we took the field for practice, that is when I first saw Richard Anthony.

He was over six foot tall; he was becoming a sophomore at our High School, and he was the kid with the golden arm. I was impressed with his presence, and I was also sympathetic because I wanted to end his cockiness. If I had his height and strength, I could swear to anyone I would be a pro for many years to come.

I was batting third and watching Rick warm up on the mound as he delivered his epic fast ball. He had a serious pop to his delivery and the more I investigated his mechanics, the more I understood his flaws. I asked everyone in the dugout to huddle around me while Rick warmed up.

"I want everyone to look at him out there and see what I see. See how he quickly looks down and then heads into his delivery? He is all arm strength guys and there is an easy way to defeat him. Make him throw pitches and earn those strikes. As you can easily see, he is wild and has the knack to overthrow", I stated to the guys.

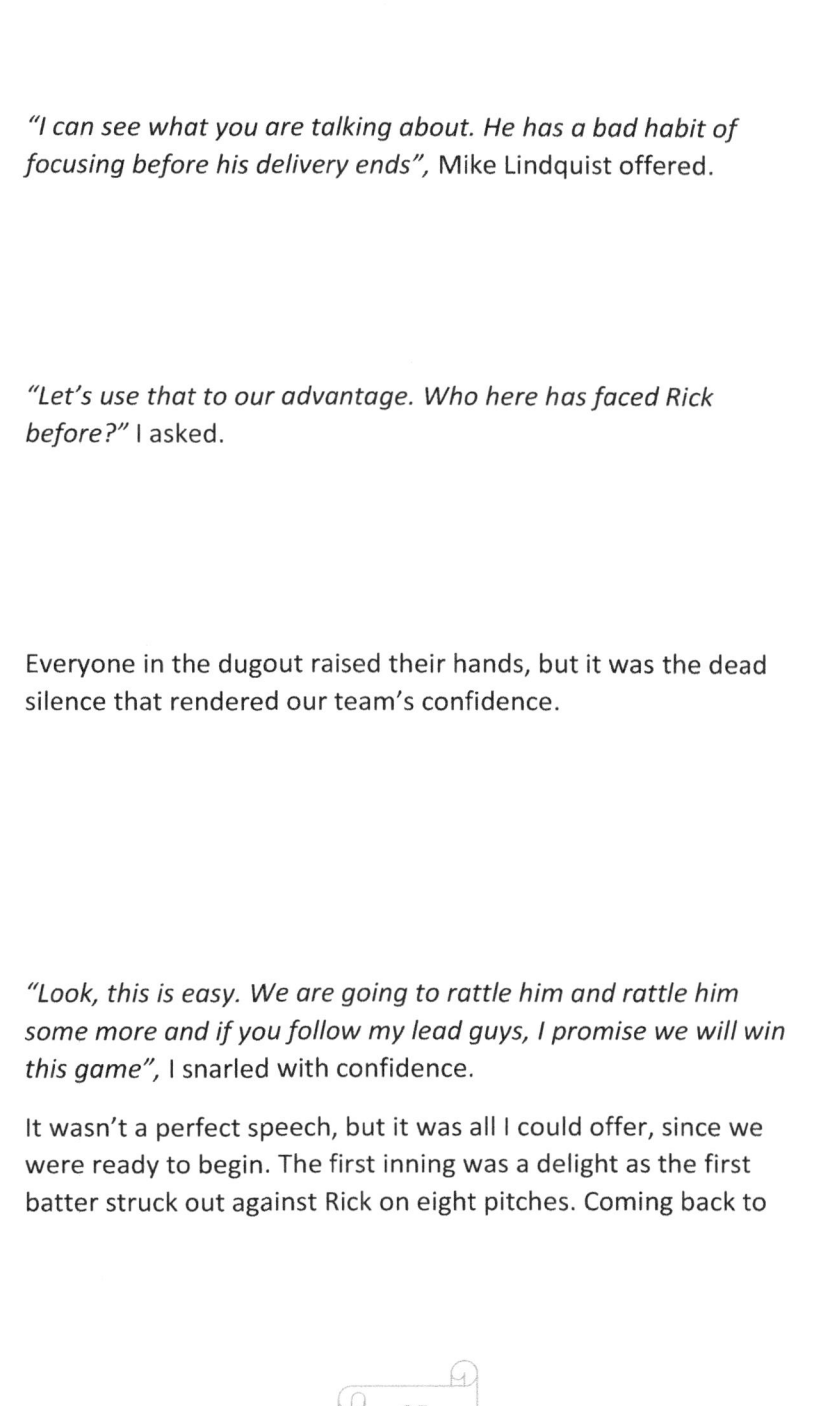

"I can see what you are talking about. He has a bad habit of focusing before his delivery ends", Mike Lindquist offered.

"Let's use that to our advantage. Who here has faced Rick before?" I asked.

Everyone in the dugout raised their hands, but it was the dead silence that rendered our team's confidence.

"Look, this is easy. We are going to rattle him and rattle him some more and if you follow my lead guys, I promise we will win this game", I snarled with confidence.

It wasn't a perfect speech, but it was all I could offer, since we were ready to begin. The first inning was a delight as the first batter struck out against Rick on eight pitches. Coming back to the dugout, Andy smiled with a confidence for the team to share. The next batter was Mike Lindquist, and he was able to squeeze a single through the first and second baseman. Rick was already ten pitches into the game before he faced his toughest competitor. Leaving the on-deck circle for the batter's box, I winced for one second as I gazed into the eyes of the tall pitcher. His confidence was high, and I was bound and determined to shake his foundation with a stare from hell.

The first two pitches were curveballs and outside of the p ate. Unaware of his knowledge of my batting skills, I stepped outside of the box and looked upon the teen and his talents. I stared at him for a mere few seconds, and he smiled with a grin that began a psychological game of warfare. He was now coming with a fastball, and I was more than prepared. Mike Lindquist knew it was also coming, so he began his quest for second base via steal.

"He is stealing second base", a voice in the crowd yelled as Rick delivered his pitch from the mound.

I was in full view of its plight as the gripping of my bat hardened while my arms began to move forward. The collision occurred over the middle of the plate and the trajectory of the ball would leave the field as quick as the pitch left Rick's hand. It was a two-run bomb into Right Field and the opposite field homer produced just enough runs to relax my teammates. It was also the first set of runs Rick had given up in over a year and the night was just beginning.

After surrounding the bases and meeting the guys at home plate, I stopped in my tracks and looked back at the man on the mound. He was shaking his head and rightfully so. That was a terrible pitch and I made him pay for his bad decision. When it came time to start the bottom of the inning, I would easily mow down the first three hitters before Rick saw me in the bottom of the second. We had tacked on another run in the inning and the three-run lead was more than enough. My approach to Rick was simple, because he was a good fast ball hitter according to my teammates. My changeup was a pitch I hadn't perfected, but I was going to master it tonight and it was the first pitch Rick saw from me. His swing began as early as the sun rises from the east and it was embarrassing. Expecting a fastball, Rick nearly began a hurricane with his missed swing and now his face began turning red. The anger is what I needed because he was out of his focus and that is when the curveball would become my second pitch. The ball left my hand and began near the top of the letters on his uniform and sank quickly towards his knees.

The plight of the pitch buckled his legs to the point he withheld his swing and left the bat on his shoulder. The called strike raised his curious eyebrows upon his angry face and his patience became lost. The third pitch was an intended wasted sinker on the outside of the plate and Rick unexpectedly swung. It took me by surprise, but Rick was nearing the end of his rope and his anger took over.

The star pitcher for the Middleton team was struggling with his control and his temper, and I began a chant from the dugout. We were having fun and I sang songs from the eighties and my teammates followed. It was loud and deafening and Rick couldn't take it anymore. The score was ten to nothing and the game ended as quick as it began for the team from Topsfield. We were the elite of the league and I recall the drive home as my arm began to hurt. I had pitched brilliantly in the full seven innings, but the discomfort was cumbersome.

My parents never allowed me the proper rest for my pitching because I was always on teams with other players that could throw. For the first time in my life, I was pitching every fourth day and never took the time to heal my arm. I never knew you were supposed to ice your arm after each game. Thanks to

Coach Foreman, his advice and ice saved my arm. The use of Bengay through the first four games of the season was wearing my arm down and I needed a break. The only loss we would suffer this summer was when I took the day off and Andy Foreman was relegated to the mound. I was confident he could get us a few good innings, but it wasn't meant to be. We were destroyed quickly against the team from Ipswich. We had no reason to lose badly other than the team leader was unavailable, and I felt bad. It was all my fault and I promised myself I would take better care of my arm.

The summer was concluding, and I was either playing baseball or beginning to venture into the neighborhood of my community. I knew my freshman year was slowly approaching, but I needed time to myself. Since I was five years old, my parents managed to always live near a wooded area. Since I was not the type to just stay home, I ventured within the confines of the wooded areas and live amongst the nature it provided. I was happy and free, and it was the only time I felt safe away from my piece of shit father. Despite my allergies and allergic reaction to poison ivy, I managed to be drama free through my childhood. I may have lived a terrible life with two abusive parents, but I was able to relinquish my anger on a lot of the paths through the trees and my surroundings.

I decided to venture out of the neighborhood with a few of the kids I just met the previous few days. They were the Buffington's, and they were three brothers named John, David and Joey. I had met them when I walked around the block and we were all laughing when David fell on his ass. John was the oldest and he was a couple of years younger than me. David and Joey were barely nine and 10 years old. This group of misfits would become my dearest friends of the neighborhood and we all decided to enter the old military base.

It was a calm Saturday morning and we had already planned to climb over the large gate in front of the base. It wasn't tall enough to prevent us from getting in, but the young boys were literally monkeys. They all had amazing energy and it was nice to have someone around that could make the days go by faster. The team and I were on a fascinating win streak, and we were headed to the championship game later in the evening. The summer was a success, and I was still left with a month before school started. It was today that put me on track to do something I have never done before. It was in inclusion for an invite that had nothing to do with me, and my parents were skeptical. Before climbing over that large fence, John Buffington had told me the Varsity and Freshman teams were holding tryouts for the football team. I never thought about playing and since my dad was a giant Miami Dolphin fan, maybe I could get him off my back and play on my own.

I wanted to get my mind away from sports for a bit and venture onto the Nike Site. The kids and I climbed over the large fence, and it was amazing that I hadn't attempted this before. As much as I loved the woods, I still maintained patience. We had been living in the house for a few months and baseball took up a lot of my time, rendering me lazy for the first time.

I loved the woods, and this was going to be one hell of an adventure. Once we got past the fence, the landscape was magnificent. I was in heaven walking from building to building and seeing the remanence of history. The road from the gate centered in between two large buildings and disappeared in the brush. Both structures were abandoned and while I spent hours glorified with the surroundings, I was a bit taken back. The old base had left books and logs of their shifts and beds were still untucked in the rooms and the carpets seemed new. The walls were a bit beat up, but the remanence of a previous life rang through the air. We were venturing onto a platform of someone else's life, and it was a struggle to understand the concept. Why the fuck would you build a missile base, only to abandon it and tear it down?

It was a pleasant distraction for my crazy life, but it allowed me to witness something that placed a stain onto my heart. This was something of a disaster and the boys and I continued towards the rear of the base. I was unsure of the amount of land the base covered, but we estimated several acres.

The road leading us towards the rear of the base was covered in brush and trees. The large cracks in the concrete indicated many years of abuse, but it was the guidance we needed. Four kids walking within the confines of a mystery waiting to be discovered. Sounds nice right? Well, it was about to get complicated because we endured a large hatch in the ground towards a place we had never expected.

John noticed a large pair of metal doors with handles protruding from the ground in the middle of nowhere.

The white sand surrounding the doors was a mystery, but when we decided to pull the handles, our eyes were left wondering regardless. The steps leading below the earth brought us a curiosity to walk beneath the ground. It wasn't long before we realized the entire area underground was flooded with water. It was disappointing because we thought we had found the way to one of the missile silos on base. Befuddled with sadness, we all closed the doors and walked back towards the gate entrance. It was a big downer to realize we couldn't continue, but we had plenty of summers ahead to continue our escapades.

Chapter 5
Feed the Wolf

The Topsfield baseball team found their way towards the end of the summer as champions. With another simple victory against the dominant Middleton team, we ended the season with one loss and a hell of a reputation. Our team was young, and we were going to spend the next few years together defending the crown we deserved. With double session practices beginning for Masconomet football tomorrow, I decided to study the Varsity team and its previous records. The Topsfield Library was a couple of miles from the house, and I rode my ten-speed through the confines of the hills of Topsfield. I needed to understand the history of our football team and everything I needed was found in several yearbooks and articles in the Salem Evening News. The Head Coach of the Varsity team was Jerry Bouvier, and he was not a delight in the least. Since he took over the program in 1986, he never had a team win more than one game in the season. He had been part of the program years prior and enjoyed a little success with an eight-win team in 1984.

While I am reading the articles, I see a column in the Boston Globe terrorizing the wishbone offense that Bouvier was teaching. I was not a huge educator on the sport, but I was smart enough to remember the Tom Osbourne led teams of Nebraska running that offense to perfection. I only knew of him because of my love for the Miami Hurricanes and their influences in the mid-eighties while they battled BC, Oklahoma or Nebraska. Studying as much as I could with little time, I was under the impression the wrong offense and defense were being implemented upon the student athletes of Masco. Jerry Bouvier couldn't coach himself out of a wet paper bag, so I decided to be smart and try out for the freshman team.

The day came to attend the tryouts for the football team and its rash of shitty seasons. It was my first attempt at football, and I had no idea what I was doing honestly. In the proceeding weeks, I had watched old film of a few sports' pro teams and their Quarterbacks. It was my belief that I was to fulfill that position simply cause it related to being a pitcher on the mound. I was considered by many in town as a beast on the diamond, but I did not want to disappoint here. When it came to meeting everyone, I was introduced to Coach Swaim. He was a bit of an oddball and he claimed he used to play football in his early day. I didn't believe him, but who really gave a shit who he was. I was tickled that most of the guys from our summer baseball team were on the freshman football team. They were all surprised to see me and Mike Lindquist and Rich Crosson automatically assumed I was going to be Quarterback.

"So, ladies. Who is going to lead this team on the field?" Coach Swaim asked.

"Shawn will!" A voice in the crowd yelled.

In all fairness here, the voice was Mike Lindquist, but I pretended not to hear it.

"So, where is this, Shawn?" Coach Swaim asked again.

I stepped in front of a few of the guys and introduced myself. Upon placing the light upon myself, Coach underhanded the football into my gut and asked me to throw a pass. Holding the pigskin and laces in my hands, the ball felt soft and easy to grip. Just like a pitcher in his windup, I took a quick three step crop and planted my left foot into the grass and released the football. The perfection of a spiral was beautiful to watch, and the quick pass landed between the numbers of the awaiting receiver thirty yards away. The look of awe again coveted my presence as Coach Swaim no longer needed convincing.

"Well, we have our Quarterback it seems. What about the rest of you? Who wants to be a part of the wolfpack?" He asked.

It took me a few minutes to get what coach was saying and it made perfect sense. He was comparing me to an alpha wolf, and I was going to lead our team to its destiny. We spent most of the day getting our pads and helmets fitted and we went over a few plays with the offense. It was a mess and I complained from the get-go upon hearing about the offense and its lack of strategy. This coming from an armchair quarterback at home watching Dan Marino's success in the NFL.

"Coach? Are you expecting us to run this crappy offense with my arm?" I think we should take advantage of our speed and depth and spread the offense", I stated.

"Shawn, I am with you all the way on this, and I have to say I must run the offense as the Varsity team sees fit. We are more than just a freshman team. We are here to learn the Varsity plays so that we can blossom someday and take over next year or later", Coach Swaim exclaimed.

I stood up in the classroom and I let the coach have an earful. I had learned all about the plays within minutes of reading them in our notes and it was a disaster. The creator of both offense and defense had clearly no idea what football was about. I was befuddled and enamored at the fact someone would waste their energy and ask young students to conduct symmetry with their hands tied to their back. It was embarrassing and I was hoping my teammates understood my stance.

"Coach, I have only known you a few hours and I can see you are a smart guy. I have spent the last few weeks studying Coach Bouvier's system and I must say, I don't agree with it. We don't have the size, speed and offensive line to garner yards on the ground against larger opponents. I am one thousand percent convinced he will be fired at the end of this season or next

season. As a matter of fact, I am convinced he will win only one game this season. I am not asking you to change anything. I am asking that we get together and create a few plays to see if I am right. I have a bulldog behind me for a running back in Richie Crosson. I have a massive tight end in Dave Daniels, and I have one hell of an ugly wide receiver in John Capobianco. I promise I will get you your wins and maybe, just maybe I can lead this team to getting you that coaching spot with Varsity. What do you say?" I stated with confidence.

"We run the plays we are given, but I will work with you on a few extra. I see your point and I agree. Let's see where this season takes us", he happily replied.

We spent the next couple of weeks garnering the strength and the knowledge of Coach Bouvier's offense. The guys on the team began understanding the failures of the system and they were slowly losing patience with Coach Swaim. We all understood his job to be that of a freshman coach without a voice, but he didn't know something. He was unaware that Coach Bouvier didn't give a shit about the freshman team in the past because they hadn't won a game in 5 years. Armed with the truth, Coach Swaim decided to make a change. He would use the philosophy of Bouvier's shitty plays and make them his own. He had a Quarterback with a huge arm, and he wanted to garner the attention of the Athletic Department. For that to happen, it would have to start against North Andover in one week. Guys like Jim Broughton, Mike Lindquist, Richie Crosson, David Daniels and Mike Moynihan were going to have to pull their weight in the offense. We knew we had a killer defense without blitz schemes and speed. I converted to cornerback, and I was responsible for covering the other team's best wide receiver. I wasn't the fastest guy on the field, but I covered easily and made up with my sense for the football.

School was beginning and we were tasked with playing on Fridays while the Varsity team played on Saturdays. My first day of school was much easier this time around because I had already taken notice with others around me. I had one hell of a summer and students I have never known before began coming up to me. I felt popular, despite not fitting in with the rest of the student body. The girls in my freshman class were amazingly gorgeous and looked like models. What the hell was I doing in this school besides making a name for myself in sports? Was that going to be my only way to get others to notice me? I had to change up a few things and I decided to be the class clown. I befriended a few guys by the name of Seth Farley and Benjamin Walburn. Those two guys took a huge liking to my personality and throughout my first week, I wreaked havoc on the student body of Masconomet with my personality.

As I had explained earlier in the book, Masco was segregated into cliques and my freshman year was no exception. Since I was popular with those in baseball, I found that Richie Crosson and Andrew Foreman were safe bets to enjoy lunch with. The others at the table were more than familiar because I had played against them as well. Travis Larrabee and David Bernard were amongst the boys at the table and so was Keith Hemeon and his dumb ass brother, Daryl. These guys were easy to entertain, and I wasn't as smart as them, but I fit in quite well. I may not have worn nice clothes like the rest of the spoiled students, but that was going to be changing soon. My mother had bad taste in clothes and since Masco was a preppy school, I had to adapt. There was only so much I could do with my cheap shirts and pants before people thought I was a fucking idiot.

My classes were simple, and I was facing the curriculum with ease as everyone began talking about the weekend's game against North Andover. Not one person cared about the

Freshman team, and I wanted to easily change that. With the help of a new friend, Kenneth Felton, we discovered old tapes of North Andover and its offense. Armed with knowledge of North Andover, we brought it to the attention of our weekly practices before the Friday game. We had noticed the football team was running a power run offense with play action. While watching the tape of North Andover and Newburyport from the year before, it was crazy to see the defense stop the run without hesitation. North Andover had a defensive scheme to place their tackles in the gaps to prevent any sort of double teams. This would prevent any holes from opening. Before you know it, Newburyport was always in a third down situation with long yardage. That is where their all-state defensive end keyed on sacking the Quarterback. For Masco to be successful, we needed to defeat the long yardage situations and throw on first and second down.

"I have an idea, but it has to involve us all", Kenneth mentioned at the beginning of our team meeting.

Kenneth and I stood up in the classroom and we briefed the team in front of Coach Swaim. We were mere freshman in a

High School of the United States, and we were directing our soldiers as if we knew what lie ahead.

"Shawn and I have reviewed private film from the games of North Andover from last year and I must say, we are going to get killed on the Varsity side of things. Now, before you all get your panties in a wad, we have an idea that will garner attention", Kenneth stated.

"Some of you in this room recall many months ago a battle in Middleton that no one had seen coming. These bunch of misfits from the town of Topsfield rode in on a white horse and stole the identity from beneath the best team in the area. Do you remember than what I said? I asked you to follow me and believe in what I was preaching. I saw a flaw in their best player, and we took that info and destroyed that guy. I am asking you guys today to utilize our information and defeat this North Andover team we haven't beaten in over 5 years. Did any of you know that this team hasn't won a game since we beat this team? I am guessing no cause some of you are lost as I can see it now. Listen to what the fuck I am saying. We could show others that our team is relevant, and I promise you this. We will

beat this team and we will beat them by over twenty points. I promise", I loudly stated.

"For us to do this, we are going to need each one of you to comprehend our new offense. Are there any questions?" Ken asked.

"Are we still going to run this wishbone offense Bouvier wants us to run?" One of the students asked from the back of the class.

"I have every intention of walking out of this meeting and going straight to his office and telling him how I feel about it. Does that answer your question? Worry about what Coach Swaim and I are implementing here. Richie Crosson is going to run as hard as he can, and I need my pass catchers to break route if the coverage breaks apart. I will do what I can to escape and improvise. Remember this team. I am dropping back for no longer than two point five seconds before the ball is released. If *time exceeds that point, then I am scrambling. You need to find me or break from the pattern and come back. Do not have me throwing the god damn ball across the field. We could create less mistakes by shoring up with our game plan and making easier plays. We are not going to be able to run the ball without establishing our pass game. It is imperative we limit the gap control and keep their linebackers honest"*, I replied.

The players were in good hands and with an excellent week of practice, Friday was upon us, and we were set to take the field at home. The time spent at school and football helped keep me away from my father, but he was out of town the entire time. He was in school somewhere in the south and for all I gave a shit, maybe he was in hell learning to become a better parent. Despite that, once the school bell rang nearing the end of school, the students immediately gathered in the locker room for the game. The downside of playing on the freshman team was the inconvenience of time. It was going to take no time at all to rush from the end of school and into our lockers. The Varsity games were on weekends, and they had time to eat breakfast, lounge around and get blown out by their opponent. We saw this as an opportunity of adversity, and we were going to crush it.

The game was to start at four in the afternoon and once the other team arrived, we had a few minutes to warm up. We decided against a team captain because we were a team and we made decisions together. We sent Ken Felton to the middle of the field to win the coin toss and defer the ball to the second half. Here was a good kid walking towards the fifty-yard line with one shoe on. Ken was our field goal kicker, and he was emulating the great kicker from the New England Patriots, Tony Franklin. Both were fucking nuts and it was a great ploy to psych the other team out while our player was literally barefoot.

We were anxious to send our defense onto the field. Against the small offensive line of North Andover, we could bully them up and down the field, and that is what we did. The first three drives for their team provided no offense and negative yardage. When our team was able to take over, Richie Crosson and I began operating the offense like surgeons in an ER. Our first three drives culminated in fourteen points and nearly two hundred yards of offense. John Capobianco was the recipient of two touchdown catches in the first quarter and by halftime, the route was on. North Andover had no answer for the offense we had mastered because they were anticipating Bouvier's crappy schemes. It was a most victorious beginning for Masco's freshman team winning 42-6. Five touchdown passes eclipsed the previous freshman record and we had Bouvier's attention.

We were considered Zombies to the head coach because he accused our team of neglecting the game plan. The great news was he supported our right to make a choice and Mister Plumley agreed and allowed our freshman team to consider retaining our changes. We knew if the athletic director stood behind us, then we had helped give Masco the reason to fire Bouvier during or after the season.

Despite our huge victory, we still had to dress up for the Saturday morning Varsity game and sit on the bench. I was psyched to know that I would probably enjoy watching a horror flick over watching Masco's Varsity team take it up the ass against North Andover. Despite my feelings, many members of the varsity team came to some of us and offered congratulations on making a stand. We weren't sure what they meant, but it was something easily taken. We earned their respect and as soldiers, we sat and watched Masco take it in the chin over and over during the first few games of the season. While the freshman team was winning by large margins, the varsity team was suffering horrific defeats. Rumors began to spread throughout the school that Bouvier was being fired at the end of the season.

Coach Swaim was excited for the opportunity, but the rumor hurt his ego. He was a small-time teacher in the community that was becoming friendlier with the administration in the athletics department. His name was Mister Pugh and he garnered attention apparently because his younger brother was a highly successful football coach in New Hampshire. Despite the words, the freshman team was standing at 5-1 and the varsity team was at a miserable 0-6. The losses were piling up and it got so bad, I was asked to quarterback the varsity team for an entire practice. Talk about taking over a sinking ship or walking onto the battlefield without a weapon. Bouvier was out of control, and I had enough of his shit, and I let him have it one afternoon on the practice field.

"No coach! No more of this! You are asking Phil to hand off to three slow running backs behind an offensive line that isn't a run block line. Can't you see if you take Lee Spencer and some of your other quick receivers and run these quick screens, you better the odds of getting a first down", I shouted.

"Hell no. This is my offense son. Don't you get it? We are going to run this play until it is done right!" He yelled.

I rolled my eyes and handed the ball back to Phil Richardson and walked towards the freshman team.

"Where are you going son?" He yelled.

I turned around in frustration and said, *"With all due respect coach, I rather be over here with a winning team"*.

I turned around and walked into the offensive huddle of our freshman team. I had taken a stand and the rest of the varsity respected me after that day. I was right in a lot of ways, but I felt bad for the students who stood behind his terrible antics. He wasn't fired weeks later, along with the rest of his terrible staff. I had taken a stand, but at what cost?

I led our freshman team to a 7-2 mark, and I was removed from the team because I took a stand. The morning after the confrontation, Mister Plumley was sent to my homeroom class and informed me of my removal from the Football team.

I knew it was Bouvier who got me removed, but I didn't care. Jim Broughton would lead our team into a tie for the final game and we didn't lose. Those guys deserved to be among the best and for a season, they were. There was never going to be another freshman team as awesome as we were, especially when our two losses were by a combined 4 points. We were nearly perfect in every way, and I was glad to be a part of the team. I was proud of the accomplishments and when it came time to choose a winter sport for the year, I wanted to glide into Basketball. The one issue I had was the coach of the varsity team. His name was Coach Kasey and his relationship with Bouvier chased me to a sport that I never thought I would become a part of.

Baseball season was arriving in the upcoming spring, so I needed the opportunity to stay far away from my family. The options were limited, and I most definitely didn't want to be a wrestler because I thought the attire was fruity. I didn't respect the Basketball coach and his miserable philosophy, so I was left with a decent option for the Indoor Track team. I was only fourteen years old, but I was in the greatest shape of my life, and it was exciting to exercise and remain strong for the upcoming spring season. The tryouts were approaching and being a Friday, everyone in the cafeteria seemed to be in a cheery mood. Normally Fridays were the day everyone anticipated the weekend and the football games, but this was a different season.

Masco's wrestling teams were traditionally good, despite their over aggressive coach in Mister Puleo. The basketball team had a few good players, but their team chemistry and coach were a mess. I chose the one sport that I could provide the most help and we had a good team. I was the true freshman that provided a spark in the football team that was mostly blamed for Coach Bouvier and his staff sporting a one-win season. A lot of the seniors didn't like me, but that was a jealousy much deserved. I didn't give a shit what they thought and if I could provide a difference in the school, then so be it.

The hatred for me as a person carried over into the cafeteria. Our table was near the back entrance, and we had a group of kids a couple of tables over causing trouble. I generally didn't have issues with anyone in school, but the gang of smokers were pissing me off. It was a collection of dumb asses who bullied weaker kids, smoked pot, used drugs, listened to Heavy Metal, disobeyed everything and hung out near the smoke tree in the parking lot of school. I am referring to Brian Woodbury, Bryce Rapson and a few others involved in the alternative program of school. Let's define alternative, shall we. Mister Pugh oversaw these fucking idiots who were troublemakers and alternatively needed help. Despite their shortcomings, I couldn't wrap myself around this group of morons. It was obvious the school needed them so we could survive among the drama, but on this beautiful Friday afternoon, I provided more fireworks.

Chapter 6
My Own Prison

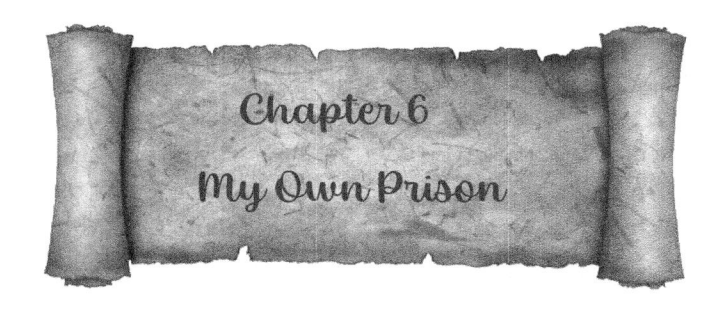

On this magnificent Friday, I sat near the guys at our table in the cafeteria. A lot of noise came from the smoker's table, and I was not in the mood. I had previously run into one of these bean poles in the hallways and knocked him to the ground. For some odd reason, they didn't like me, and I didn't like them. Despite the mutual feelings, there were a lot of these fuckers, and I had no interest in beating up on an army of skinny alternative dumb asses. With my mood on edge, some of the guys at our table were rolling their eyes at the collection of dumb fucks and their antics. While looking over towards their table, an orange flew into my direction and I luckily caught it, preventing Dave Bernard from getting smashed in the face. I had enough, so I stood up and threw the orange in a different direction. My arm was quick, and I threw the small fruit at a speed still undefined as it landed against the wall. Splattering across the wall and floor, Brian Woodbury and a few of his friends stared into my direction. Their intentions fell short, but they took notice of my problem with them.

Several minutes passed and as I began walking out of the cafeteria, the same group was waiting for me in the hallway.

"Get that son-of-a-bitch", Brian shouted.

The group awaiting my arrival consisted of five teens dressed in Metallica and different heavy metal shirts. Their long goofy hair and terrible postures stood in the shadows, while my conscience made a quick decision. I knew I was one of the fastest teens in the building, so I began running down the hall towards the Junior High area. I knew they couldn't follow me for long while wearing their tight jeans and cheap tennis shoes. Their heavy hairspray weighed them down and the fear turned into excitement as I yelled happily. These slow ass knuckleheads didn't bare a chance of catching me and I smiled as I ran faster.

"God damn that guy is fast", one of my chasers yelled.

Within seconds, I had built a tremendous lead over the five smokers and found myself in a field between the High School and Junior High buildings. I am not going to lie here and say I wasn't afraid. I had been severely beaten and nearly died by a group of teens, so that rested in the back of my mind. I had no idea how dangerous these idiots were, but I was on high alert for the rest of the day and possibly the school year.

I had no other issues the rest of the day and my tryout for the indoor track team was an easy success. Despite the rough day, I was able to enjoy a little confidence and I brought it home for the weekend celebration. My family was invited to a small party at one of our neighbors' houses for the weekend. The Keeton's were a military family that had lived in the neighborhood a little longer than us. Keith was a devoted husband to his wife Marla, and they took a special liking to my sister. I was busy with school and sports to really care that my sister was spending a tremendous amount of time at the Keeton house. Armed with that knowledge, I attended the party on a brisk Saturday afternoon. I wasn't attempting to give much attention to the Keeton's and their weird ways of garnering attention. I had asked to use the restroom and as the evening was winding down, I heard a few noises from the back bedroom. The commotion wasn't anything alarming, but Keith's voice was deep and subtle. While using the restroom, I quietly attempted to observe the conversation.

I could swear I heard my sister's voice saying that she didn't want to do anything he asked. Maybe I misheard, but it was most definitely my sister and Keith apparently wanted to ravage the young twelve-year-old. Something clearly was inappropriate, and I immediately brought it to the attention of my mother. Terri Wallis was a woman who could talk your ears off with strange innuendos and calming theories, but this had to top the cake. Upon telling my mother what occurred, she paused for a moment and then offered a ridiculous reaction.

"Go home now and wait for your father", she yelled with a cigarette in her mouth.

What the fuck was this woman thinking? Her daughter is in the back room being propositioned by a man triple her age and she clearly didn't give a shit. The one thing that did happen was the fearful anger her husband portrayed on me. Earlier the day before, I was chased by 5 morons in tight jeans and today, I was being chased by the one man who wanted to kill me. Gary Wallis got wind of the accusation and upon upsetting my mother, that was the invitation he needed. He quickly left the Keaton house and chased me up the street and grabbed me from behind. The walk to our house was brief, since the Keaton's lived a couple of houses down the road. When Gary was able to catch up, we were standing in our yard in front of the house. He immediately began swinging his fists and landing them upon my face. I wanted to defend myself and beat the crap out of the little man that called himself my father. He was a fraud and since I was able to take a beating like Rocky Balboa, I did little to stop this psycho.

The punches were extreme, and he knocked me to the ground in front of our large bay window of the living room. My head lay against the cold grass as he began sitting on my chest and whaling on me with his arms. Gary Wallis was not a large man standing barely over five feet. He was a wrestler in his High School, so he thought he was a tough guy beating on his frail son. If I wanted, I could have easily knocked him over and threw him through the window, but why? Why would I attempt to beat up my fake father when he was someday going to face punishment for what he was doing. I was biding my time and just when the thought crossed my mind, Gary grabbed a large stone from behind my head and raised it above his own. Holding both hands on the football sized rock, the evil upon the eyes of the man who was supposed to be my protector, grew black.

In a matter of seconds, one of the neighbors tackled Gary off me and into the ground. The rock fell just below my feet and the neighbor across the street phoned the police. Standing up on his feet, Gary let me have it vocally.

"You have embarrassed me and your mother for the last fucking time Shawn. You ever do that again, I will fucking kill you", he screamed.

His own words frightened the neighbors and as the police arrived, Gary knew he fucked up. Beating your own son in front of his yard was one of the stupidest things a parent could do. The police immediately grabbed him and placed him in the back of the car. The commotion in the front of our yard presented a dramatic beginning for all the neighbors to witness. They all felt bad for me, but none of them knew the real reason for the beating. My own selfish parents didn't care about their daughter being molested by the neighbor, so I had to become the victim of my sister's molestation. I wanted my father to knock Keith out and put him in prison for a long time. How in the world can a family man molest a young girl and get away with it? Would you believe that Keith Keaton was never prosecuted for molesting my sister during our time in Topsfield?

I had the ability to prevent a huge crime against my sister, but instead, I was the victim of a savage beating that nearly ended my life. It was this evening that destroyed any relationship I had with my sister, mother or piece of shit father. The drinking was taking his mind over and the police offered him an ultimatum that day. Stop the drinking or go to jail and lose his career in the Coast Guard. It was an easy decision for Gary Wallis, and this was the day we would give up drinking forever. Maybe this was going to change him into a better person, and I was hoping so for my sake.

My Friday started off dramatic and the weekend didn't get any better. I was now estranged from my loser father and my mother had lost all respect. The whispers of the neighbors created friction with everyone, and we seemed to be a family on an island. Nothing against me, but not one family in the Nike Site wanted to befriend my parents. They were selfish as they could be, and they deserved the grumblings from others.

Winter was slowly passing us over and before we all knew it, spring arrived, and the school year was now in full baseball mode. I was unaware of baseball tryouts, so I was not able to attend any opportunities to join the varsity or junior varsity teams. The freshman team was comprised of a lot of the same teens I had already played with the previous summer. His name was Coach Bettencourt, and he was just as drunk as my father. He was a large burly man with a rough beard, huge pot belly filled with fire and the desire to win. I liked him a lot and he was not shy when it came to his pride and baseball. Coach was a lonely man and he saw something in me that Coach Foreman saw, and he immediately knew what he had. We basically almost fielded the same team as we did in the Summer League, but we had a few exceptions. Some of the players from the Middleton and Boxford teams were now sharing the roster with us. The Masco freshman baseball team was built to win, and we could basically take down anyone at any time.

Players from the varsity team were asking their coach to include me on their team, since they were needing a pitcher. When I heard the rumblings in school, I had no desire to play on the team. I was happy with my situation and when I found out that we would be scrimmaging the junior varsity team, I was elated. It was our world series, and we anticipated the older kids to give us their best. The freshman team had their home games at Proctor Park in downtown Topsfield, and it was a delight for me. I was undefeated on that mound and the JV team had no idea what they were in for. During earlier practices, I noticed my fastball becoming faster and crisper. The team we were facing was comprised of mostly sophomores and a couple of rejected players from the varsity team.

I didn't have time to study a lot of the players and Coach Bettencourt announced I would lead our team onto the diamond. The team we were facing assumed they would roll over their opponent, but they picked the wrong day. I had struck out the first ten batters I had faced with my electric fastball and enormously amazing curve ball. I was on fire and Coach Bettencourt had saw something in me that other coaches didn't. Our schedule was filled with fifteen games spaced over a four-day resting period in between each game. Coach thought he could start me all season in every game and flirt with a chance at perfection. I was on board with his philosophy and our defense wasn't the strong suit of our team. We had one of the most prolific offenses in Masco history and we didn't have much of a weakness in our lineup. Our offense was on pure display in the scrimmage against the JV team.

Christopher Powers was the pitcher tasked with the impossible against our lineup that afternoon. He was a senior reject that couldn't handle the plateau from the varsity team, as he was relegated to handling pitching duties on the irrelevant JV team. I was never a fan of the junior varsity concept because if you couldn't make the varsity team, you had no business playing at all. I couldn't understand the concept, but here we were, and Christopher Powers was our first victim. Since they were considered the home team in our game, I was tasked with batting third in front of two singles. Chris had a weak fastball, and he was attempting to locate the pitches on the outer corner of the plate. The issue he inherited was his location and his poor arm strength. If you were going to blow a pitch past me, it had to be delivered with confidence and this kid had zero. The walk I had been given was a blessing for him as our team would register a total of eight runs in the first three innings. Coach Bettencourt and his staff had seen enough, and we called the game due to mercy. The fifteen hits were prescribed as vicious in the eyes of the JV team, but they were in over their heads. We weren't cocky enough to call for a scrimmage against the varsity team, because we knew we were better. We knew what we were capable of, and we took that confidence into a miraculous season. The Spring of 1988 brought misery to the varsity and JV baseball teams, but the lone success lied on the arm of the one teen who would transform his pitches into one of the State of Massachusetts best pitchers for years to come.

We had completed the season in fashion with a 14-1 record, with our lone loss against Newburyport earlier in the year. Coach Sauchuk had a lot to look forward to for his varsity team and the rumors throughout school developed a championship team for the future.

During the baseball season, I had developed a dislike for my bullies and their friends. On a day-to-day basis, I was fighting these fuckers away from locations in the hall and during lunch. My friends didn't understand how I could handle the adversity and the daily struggle, but I was fearless. None of my friends knew I was a product of child abuse my entire life and they didn't know about my beating at my previous school. I had a heart of stone, and I was just your average teen who loves sports, listened to Cinderella, Motley Crue, and Winger and loved music more than life itself. I have a huge diverse choice of music from country to rock and it allowed me the chance to understand fantasies.

I would imagine being a drummer in a concert or the lead singer of the band and performing for millions while taking a shower at home. I had huge aspirations, and it leveled my anxiety a bit as I fought my bullies from time to time. The end of the year was no exception and a friend of mine had informed me of a plot from a few teens to jump me after my exams were concluded. When I got wind of that, I decided to skip the Spanish class exams and venture into the woods near the school. I wasn't ready to endure another near-death experience, so I avoided the issue. Since we lived several miles from Masco, I invited myself to skip school and walk home. It was the last day of the year, so who gave a shit, and besides, I was avoiding a conflict. I may have been delaying the inevitable, but I was alive and well and about to enjoy my summer.

The summer of 1989 was a springboard into my sophomore year, and I had a lot of decisions to make. Would I make the leap to the varsity teams in both baseball and football? It all depends on the hiring by the Athletic Director and who was going to lead our football team. We were atrocious on the field, and I am sure the alumni were tired of the losing seasons. I had a few months to endure those changes, but the summer was mine and I wanted to do something to be different. My freshman year brought a huge positive and negative spotlight upon me, and a change was going to do me well.

The first change to occur was my fucking embarrassing wardrobe. I dressed like one of the kids from the partridge family and for me to become a part of the school, I needed better clothing. There was a kid in our class named Andy Washburn and I loved how he looked good in Ralph Lauren. I told my parents how I was going to achieve buying the Polo shirts and corduroy pants with my own money. I needed a job, and my mother helped me find a McDonalds location in Danvers looking for a full-time employee. I was excited to interview for the position and without much experience, the manager hired me on the spot. Since this was a busy restaurant location, my lack of experience was easily manageable. I had a great personality, and I was now going to manage a full schedule of summer baseball, Nintendo, and work. I was growing up fast and was barely home to suffer the abuse my father missed giving me. Trust me when I say this people, it was going to eventually come back to me tenfold.

I was working relentlessly at McDonald's every day it seemed, and the reward was priceless. I was gaining experience, money, new friends and freedom from my abusive household. My sister was still visiting the Keaton's house on occasion and at this point, since my parents didn't care, I followed suit. There was a lot going on and I was extremely busy to the point I forgot about my upcoming double sessions for football. Bouvier was still the coach and he brought on a new assistant to help spice up his struggling play calling. I was confident enough to understand I was going to be riding the bench and I didn't care. Phil Richardson was our team's QB, and he was going to have a horrible offensive line and crappy offense to contend with.

The summer played me like a zombie in ways I could never imagine. We would dominate the baseball league once again as it cemented my reputation as a dominant pitcher. I yielded one earned run all summer and I was on fire at the plate with a batting average above six hundred. The competition was scarce at best and with a job, baseball and a plethora of daily activities, I was tired. I realize being fifteen has its advantages, but I was preparing for my second year of High School and didn't want to lean on my parents. I saved enough to buy an entire wardrobe of new clothes and the Marshalls in Peabody was calling my name. Who could ever sympathize with a young teen and his ability to enjoy shopping? Can you say keeper for any lucky lady in the future?

Andrew Washburn was on my mind, and I was specific towards the clothes I wanted. Within a few minutes of walking through the doors of Marshalls, I had already picked a long sleeve Pink Polo Oxford button down and another in green. I would finally locate two others in yellow and blue. The corduroy pants were a huge fashion up here in Boston and I was delighted to grab three pairs. Upon picking a few pairs of shoes, I had given myself the ability to finally fit at Masco, and that is what I did. The first day of school put a huge smile on my face and despite having to become a possible player under Coach Bouvier, he did me a solid in return. I was announced as the starting QB for the JV team and the entire freshman team from the year before would play with me. Despite Coach Swaim's mental toughness, he was no longer coaching, and I took a lot of flak for it. The new coach of the junior varsity team was also the assistant coach behind Bouvier. This was going to be a difficult year and not all the talent of Dan Marino could save our season. We were doomed before it began, and it all started with our first game.

We spent a good portion of the summer learning this terrible offense. It was misguided, broken and lost and we had to try to utilize it. Coach Bouvier knew I was a critic and he punished me by having his coaches watch over me. It was his persistence in this offense to watch me struggle and I did mightily. The first few games were double digit losses and we struggled to run the ball. The junior varsity opponents had already drawn a play book to stack the boxes against us. We were facing eight- and nine-man fronts, and Bouvier's wishbone scheme sucked. Against Newburyport, we were winning by a score of 13-0 and we were on their five-yard line. Before I go any further, lets chat about our score and how we were able to put points on the board.

I opened the game with a one-hundred-yard return for a score on the kickoff. We had practiced our special teams returns and I was tired of listening to the bullshit from our coach. He was a fucking idiot like his boss, and I took the ball from the goal line and faked hard to the right and then maneuvered left along the sideline for the score. I easily ran a 4.6 second forty time and it was with relative ease that I scamper along the sideline for the easy score. The second score came from a defensive touchdown on a fumble recovery. This was our only scoring so far and we were on the verge of an offensive touchdown. The play I was asked to perform was a dive through the stacked box. I didn't like the play call on first down, but I proceeded. As I had anticipated, we were stuffed hard and lost one yard. With second down on the horizon, the play came in as the same as before.

"What the fuck?" I yelled in the huddle.

"How can we win anything with these shit plays he is calling?" Richie Crosson asked.

"Guys, I will audible at the line. We all go on the first hut", I commanded.

Despite how the coaches felt about me, the players were on my side. We were congruent to my philosophy and if they had listened to me the year before, these coaches would be still here for many years to come. We broke from the huddle and while I read the defense, we were in formation to run through the heart of their stacked linebackers. I noticed they were initiating man coverage on my left, meaning I could audible the offense to a simple slant pattern and walk in the endzone.

I audibled a slant play for my outside wide receiver, and just as I finished my cadence, you could hear the shouting from our sidelines. Coach was mad and just as I threw the ball from behind the offensive line, the projection of the ball landed between the numbers of our receiver. The touchdown was well earned, and we accomplished a feat we were proud of. The Coach disagreed with the way we scored and benched me for the remainder of the game. I knew then I was finished with Masco football, and I found myself walking off the field and into the locker room to collect my belongings. No one else was around while the team was in the third quarter on this Monday evening. I wasn't paying much attention, but I was surprised by three teens I had recognized. I was in the middle of changing and I was bare naked with my white ass exposed to the elements of the locker room. Covered in sweat, Duane White, Jody Lane, and their butt-buddy Craig reach over to grab me as Duane punched me in the face. The hit stung a bit and it put me in a daze as the boys struggled to turn me over. Naked as the day I was born, Jody grabbed a baton from his jacket and began smashing me over the back. I was unable to move because my face was supplanted on the bench as my bare knees were on the ground. I was bent over and primed for these boys to do whatever they wanted. I was strong, but these guys were stronger together. Jody and Duane swapped positions and all I could see were the splinters of the old wooden bench.

Craig held my head as Jody sat on my back and Duane grabbed the baton and began shoving it into my rectum. The pain was horrendous and with each thrust, my ass split wide open in agony. I was now being raped by three teens that were supposed to be my classmates and it reminded me of Uncle Frank.

I was in a daze and the rape occurred for nearly sixty seconds before Duane took the baton and bashed me in the back of the head.

"That's for Brian you pussy. Don't ever forget who own's your ass now", Duane whispered in my ear as he slammed my face into the bench.

I was left lying on the ground, my rectum bleeding and my body bruised. The game outside of the locker room was hardly completed, but my body was broken. My soul was bent, and I slowly crawled back on my feet and walked over towards the showers, tears streaming from my eyes. Each step towards the shower was painful as my ass, head and body were limp. The warm shower disguised my falling tears as Duane White, Jody Lane and their friend Craig raped me to the point of no return, and I wanted to die. Contemplating hanging myself at the shower stall, I broke down as I lay helpless under the hot shower. I wanted to tell everyone what happened, but I would be ridiculed for the rest of my life. I was a hero to a lot of these classmates of mine and the moment I showed I was broken; I could lose everything. Laying on the floor in misery and drowning in fear, I felt as if I was trapped in my own prison. Garnering the strength to move away from the damage, I had to fight on and tell someone. How could these boys get away with hurting someone and not attempting this one anyone else. I knew this was revenge for what I had done last year, but I didn't deserve the cruelty or callousness of the crime. What did I do so wrong to these guys? What could I have possibly done so wrong for them to strip the sanctity of my own freedom?

I attempted to wash away the pain and the hurt as the water slowly guided itself through my pores. The sins of my anguish slowly rinsed through the drain in the floor, and I limped quickly back to my locker. It was mere minutes before the team would come back and I didn't want them to see me. I was retiring from the football team, and I relegated myself to something I had never wanted to become. It was getting late; it was a Monday and I needed time to prepare my rouse. I was cunning enough to develop a way to get my story out, but I had to be tricky. I wanted revenge on the boys who nearly murdered me a few years ago and now I wanted revenge on these three cowards.

I wanted to break down everyone that hurt me and before I could, I had a surprise for the ages. I was going to wreak havoc on the souls of the teens that penetrated my body and make their lives miserable. I remember John Buffington mentioning a single father living in our neighborhood who was a bad ass. He was a Navy Seal who was a trainer for younger fighters, and I needed to talk with him. Maybe this was bad timing, but I needed to prepare for the fight of my life. This was going to take time and I needed a distraction like no tomorrow. I settled in at home and thought through the night of my plight to get my revenge. I called my friend Jeffrey Ames, and he reminded me of a kid in our school that was kicked off the football team for using steroids.

He needed money, and I broke down and shared with Jeff what happened to me in the locker room. He was able to convince me of this new student and his ability to help. With Jeff's guidance and friendship, I offered the new student a total of two hundred dollars to beat up Duane White. This was the temporary distraction I needed and within days, the fight occurred, and Duane took the beating of his life. The student in question was a well-built machine with muscles and he could fight like the dickens. Upon hurting Duane and knocking him to the ground, he got on one knee and whispered a demand inside of his ear. Jeffrey shared that information with me, and Duane was not happy. He had known I was behind the beating, and I assumed I was going to face more wrath in the future. With that in mind, I did the one thing I could, preventing further turmoil. I took it upon myself to walk over to the fifth house on the block and present my situation in hopes that I could be trained to protect myself. John Buffington mentioned he was a trainer of self-defense, and I was going to do everything I could to find out. I had known about the guy since I met John and his brothers in the neighborhood, but rumors were meant to distract people from reality.

Knocking on the door was one thing but standing in front of a Navy Seal was another. When I reached over to slam my knuckles on the wooden door, I had an epiphany. What the fuck was I doing? I was Shawn Wallis, and I needed more time to understand what I was doing. What better time than now to learn how to defend myself. I was now away from football, and I had a couple of months before track began. Before I could walk away and run, the door opened slowly.

"Hi, what can I do for you young man?" He asked.

"Hi. My name is Shawn, and I am here looking for your help", I stated.

"I think you have me confused son. I really don't need anything at this time", he replied.

"That isn't what I meant. I need your help because I was recently assaulted by three boys at school and a few years ago, I was

nearly killed by a group of teens", I stated as I bit my lip in anticipation.

I didn't want to tell him the truth about what happened at school in fear he would think I was a pussy. More than anything, I was looking for someone to respect my issues.

"I am so sorry that happened to you. What is it that you need from me, though?" He asked.

"I was told by someone that you train other teens and adults to defend themselves. Is that correct or is he wrong?" I asked.

"Your name is Shawn, right? Well, it appears you are here seeking revenge and I think that is the wrong thinking here and I don't encourage it", he mentioned.

"I am sorry to have bothered you. All I wanted was the chance to learn how to defend myself", I cried out.

"What are you wanting me to say here? I teach kids and adults to better their understanding of life and the balance it takes to manage it. I do teach people to defend themselves, but revenge is not the way to start. You have a lot of hate inside of you Shawn and before I can help, you need to go back home and work your way from the hatred", he commanded.

"I respect your wishes and I am sorry I interrupted your day. Take care sir", I mentioned as I walked away through the neighborhood.

John's advice was incorrect, and I was back at square one. I walked around the neighborhood with my sore ass and bruised ego and began jogging. Step by step, I fought the pain and remained calm as I allowed the air to guide me. From a slower pace to a much quicker pace, I found myself running through the neighborhood like a free bird. It was exciting, my breathing was crisp, and I was alive for the first time in a while. I had classmates that ran cross country, and I could never understand the purpose until now. They felt alive, free and a part of something magical. In my entire life, I never took the time to run free and here I was, escaping my issues. I had taken the time to run up the hill on one side of the neighborhood and my legs felt stronger and tighter. Once I had conquered the hill, I approached the street before the entrance to the Nike Site and as I slowed my pace, a familiar person stepped onto the roadway.

"How do you feel now?" The stranger asked.

"Much better", I murmured while breathing heavy and placing my hands and arms behind my head.

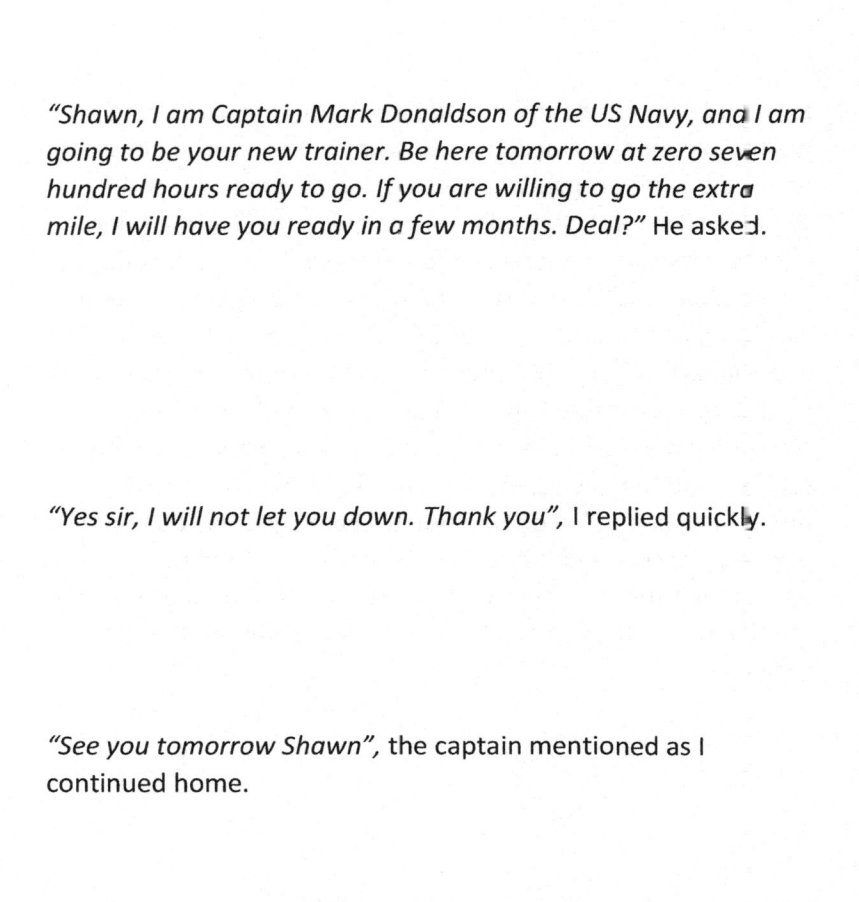

"Shawn, I am Captain Mark Donaldson of the US Navy, and I am going to be your new trainer. Be here tomorrow at zero seven hundred hours ready to go. If you are willing to go the extra mile, I will have you ready in a few months. Deal?" He asked.

"Yes sir, I will not let you down. Thank you", I replied quickly.

"See you tomorrow Shawn", the captain mentioned as I continued home.

Each foot quickly running home, I felt alive, and my body was beginning to withstand the bruising and the pain. I was battered beyond repair, but my heart was beating strong. I was going to learn how to defend myself and I was confident enough in my own heart to become a better fighter.

Chapter 7
The Darkness Settles in....

The friendly neighbor must have known the rumblings about me through the Nike Site rumor mill. Here was this torn young man who was nearly killed in his front yard by his piece of shit father. I somehow thought he was wanting to help me because of that, but as I arrived at his front door at seven in the morning, the darkness began to settle in.

The captain let me into his home and his daughter wasn't around for the weekend. He explained he lived alone mostly but had his daughter on occasion as he was going through a divorce. I made myself comfortable on the couch and the memorabilia on the walls stood out. Large paintings of the Battle at Gettysburg took up an entire section of the living room. The view was spectacular and staring deep into the painting, it felt alive. If you want me to be honest here, the guy's house was in mint condition and there wasn't a speck of dust anywhere. I wasn't used to that because I had a lazy mother in our house, and we had dog hair everywhere. I was thinking to myself, why would a Navy Captain be living in this low economy housing? I understood why my family lived here since both my selfish parents spent sixty percent of their income on cigarettes and alcohol.

"Shawn. I need you to listen closely. I am doing this for you because I don't want to see you get hurt anymore. I grew up in a very strict household in Japan on a military base and I had to learn discipline before honor. Are you familiar with Kata?" He asked.

"I have never heard of it. Are you talking about something like the Karate Kid?" I asked with a giggle.

"Yes. Something like that. Remember when Mister Miyagi trained Daniel with all those maneuvers and defense techniques?" He asked.

"Wax-on, wax-off. Right?" I replied.

"Sure. It was a defensive strategy for Daniel to defend himself when others were to attack. I want to teach you to defend yourself, build your strength and withstand any more of these beatings. Shawn, I heard you are a phenomenal athlete and with a little more discipline, you can really change things for yourself. Are you sure you are ready?" He asked.

"Yes, sir I am", I replied with confidence.

"I want you to start running five miles a day. I spent the time to measure the circumference of the neighbor road and if you circle it twice, it equals the distance of one mile. I want you to start with ten laps and stop after", he dictated.

I walked out his front door and sat on top of the cool grass and began stretching. All I could think about was those fucking buffoons at school and their bullyish mentality. I couldn't believe this was all because of that day in the cafeteria last year. I relegated my current situation to that of a prison. I was succumbing to the bully of the yard, and I was allowing others to take advantage. The captain was right, and I had to fight for myself and end this bullying. With that in mind, I gathered my balance, stood on my feet, placed my headphones upon my ears, inserted the Rocky IV soundtrack, pressed play, and began running. The duration of my jog strengthened my legs and I never felt tired. The cool morning air was a freshness my lungs needed, and I felt invincible with each step. Thoughts of South Weymouth and Masco rendered my feelings moot as I began running harder through the neighborhood. I had this anger deep inside as I recollected the beatings and I started to lose focus. My breathing slowed my pace, and I knew this would take a while to move on from. I so badly wanted to go back to Weymouth and kick the shit out of the teens who nearly killed me. Duane White and his scrawny buddies also deserved a beating, and I summoned enough strength to temper expectations.

Revenge was going to be served with a cold dish and it was just a matter of being patient. Step by step, I ran in sync with the beat of each song on the tape as if I was Rocky on the streets of Philadelphia. Upon finishing my laps, I spent the next few hours learning techniques in the back yard. The captain was attentive and very demanding when it came to training. I was only able to see him on evenings and weekends, so our training was difficult and quick. My school schedule didn't interfere as my schoolwork began to improve with better focus and attention. My parents never really gave a shit and with my grades improving, I was able to keep Gary off my ass.

For the remaining days in the Fall of 1989, I would nearly spend every waking moment with my trainer. I was becoming faster, stronger and more resilient within myself. He had mastered three different styles within the confines of Kenpo, Aikido and Taekwondo. Training was easy in the beginning, but my focus was real. Despite the changes within me, I was still fighting off the bullies at school. There was the occasional bump in the hallway that would knock them into the walls of the lockers. It wasn't just one or two of these idiots attempting to intimidate me. This was a rash of these Metallica t-shirt wearing fuck wads and I was literally stomping on four to five of these guys. It was a shock in their eyes because I was becoming a shit brick house and they were failing to scare me. The incident a few months prior in the locker room would never again come to fruition, but the attempts came in droves. In early December, Duane and his friend Craig waited for me after one of my classes.

Coincidentally, it was near my locker, and I took notice quickly. In the past, I would have done what I could to avoid them or run off and hoped they would give up chasing me. Today was going to be different because I basically walked between them, and they both just stared at each other. When they began to follow me, I just kept walking until Duane grabbed my shoulder and squeezed as hard as he could. The pain was relentless, but I ignored it and moved on like the captain advised me too. I was avoiding these bullies at every turn and as the fall turned into winter, the attacks were less and less.

I was now in my second year on the track team, and we were a force to be reckoned with. We finished with a winning record, and I found my niche in the fifty-yard hurdles. The season was

marred with plenty of controversy, but I had spent the entire winter concentrating on school, my training with the captain and the varsity track team. As you can clearly see, my picture on the track team photo was nothing to write home about. I was a mess with that curly hair, but I was getting bigger and stronger. I had gained a few inches and nearly twenty-five pounds since the school year began. Others were taking notice and the bullies weren't too far behind.

The snow fell tirelessly all winter and the season was a mess since it interfered with my training. I was in full defense mode and what began several months prior, now came to a head as I slowly learned offensive and defensive strategies. The captain was teaching me all three styles of Taekwondo, Aikido and Kenpo and these styles were vastly different, the training was brutal. I gave all I could for the man who took the time to improve my skills and it was paying off dearly.

My muscles were constantly cramping in the middle of the night and the pain was sometimes unbearable. I would wake up in agony and I hid my screams the best I could to prevent being a problem. There wasn't a day Bengay found its way onto my skin to help with the strained muscles.

"Shawn. Today you are going to learn a few techniques I know affiliated with Kenpo. The first is called a two-hand grab or Kimono grab. This is a defense against someone holding your shirt up high with two hands. Being grabbed by the shirt is one of the first aggressive postures a bully will present to you. This technique is very effective for breaking that hold, so pay close

attention. This will leave your attacker or bully second-guessing their actions once you master this. It involves a chop to the throat, an elbow sandwich to the head, a hammer fist to the crotch, and a back kick. Yeah, they'll second guess their actions again when they mess with you Shawn. You're going to start by pinning your attacker's hands against your chest with your left hand. From there, bring your right forearm down on their elbows to break their hold, shuttle into them and chop their throat, elbow smash their head, pivot and hammer fist their testicles, back kick their gut, and then walk away", he perfectly explained.

The moves were rapid and within a few minutes, I was hammering the captain and his words.

"Ok. The darkness explains this next one. This is a defense against a right sucker punch from the right side. This is good to know because no one likes a sucker punch. And this is another attack most people have experienced at some point in their lives. Although the one doing the punching always seems to be the wimpiest person with the loudest mouth, like your attackers.

It's an excellent technique to know, as well, because it teaches not just how to defend the punch but also finish the attacker off so that they can't get another strike in. Seriously, it does. An eye rake, a heel palm to the kidney, a back fist to the head, and a head sandwich. Yeah, they're not coming back at you after all that. You're going to step away from the punch and parry it away, then step around behind your attacker while raking their eye and striking their kidneys with a heel palm at the same time. From there, your right-hand forms and back fist and hits the back of their head. Kick the back of their knee with a side thrust kick to bring them to the ground. Lastly, finish them off with an elbow smash to the head", he exclaimed.

I repeated step two as much as I could and with his guidance, I was on point, and I was beginning to realize my strength came from deep within. I always had fast hands, and with a bit more resilience, I was even faster, and we are talking some Bruce Lee shit here.

"If you've never dealt with a sucker punch from the side, you may have dealt with a punch from the front, whether you knew it was coming or not. This technique offers a simple defense against such a punch, but as was the case with darkness, it also teaches how to render the attacker unable to fight back before you're away. It's a fast technique that demonstrates the quick, circular motions that Kenpo is known for, and it is simple but has a powerful finish."

This guy was good, and he was so quick and precise. I was wondering how many more combinations there were because I was getting tired. Before I could imagine another break in my mind, he kept talking. We spent the next few hours working on both techniques over and over. I was mastering it to perfection, and I was noticing the speed I was creating in both my arms and legs. Once the training was done for the day, I ran my five miles and headed home. I was both exhausted and excited to garner the ability to defend myself and provide a good offense. It was Saturday night, and I knew I had a lot more to learn on Sunday, weather permitting.

With the weekend off from the track team at school, Sunday was going to be spend all day training. I had a few more techniques to learn and when seven in the morning arrived, I was front and center with my trainer.

The defense described here is against a right punch. The technique is just as effective against a left-handed punch. You just mirror the motions, i.e., parry with your right hand instead of the left, etc. You step forward to the left as your attacker punches, parrying the blow at the same time with your left hand. From there, use your right forearm to further block the punch with an extended outward block in a circular motion and transition to grabbing their wrist. Then, right roundhouse-kick them in the body and cover away. Got all that?" He asked.

"Let me repeat", I explained as I mirrored his moves and towards the end of the exercise, I accidentally kicked him in the groin area.

"I am so sorry. I did not intend on that happening", I cried out.

"No worries, Shawn. I didn't need them anyway", he joked.

We stopped for a while as he attempted to heal his little coconuts. Snowflakes began to pierce the crisp air and before we could blink our eyes, the sky was painted white. I didn't want to stop, so we finished the last few techniques in the snow.

I was learning all types of moves to defend myself against a two- or three-person attack and overhand attacked with weapons. My trainer was amazing and brilliant at the same time, and he was proud of his student. He was now going to demonstrate the last part of Kenpo and my concentration was better than ever.

"Shawn, this last step is about you and the approaching attacker. You step forward toward the punch, block and grab the wrist with your right hand, smash the elbow with your left

hand, back fist to the ribs, palm strike to the shoulder, and take your attacker to the ground. You then jump and come down, raking both heels across their kidney, drop your knees into their spine between their shoulder blades, lift their head backward, twisting their neck to the side. Twisting the head to the side makes it easier to chop the bridge of the nose, breaking it."

From there, jump up and roundhouse-kick them in the face", he finally finished explaining.

"That seems simple. It mirrors the frontal attack, but I can see a weapon here that I can easily remove from their hand", I explained.

"Now you are on it my friend. Good job today. I want you to enjoy your Holiday and come back on the first Monday in January. I want you to begin the last stages of weapons handling and then proceed into Taekwondo", he mentioned.

I was elated to spend Christmas with my friends down the street and not worry about training for a while. I also broke ground at school when it came to learning more about the hurdles. I didn't think I was good at all, but I seriously had an idea that was going to propel me into one of the best runners in our league. The issue I noticed was with my start and form when it came to approaching the first hurdle. In the competition, the five hurdles are placed in a straight line and the start and finish lines are separated by one hundred and fifty feet. I learned the hard way to make sure my jump was in sync to prevent a massive groin injury.

Not just anyone can perfect the symmetry required to break the school record for Masconomet. The school records for the indoor track team were listed on the wall of the gymnasium and the 7.0 seconds in my event created a new focus. My freshman and sophomore years had me close at 7.2 seconds and I needed more time to master the perfect score. I was becoming faster and did just enough to help our team finish with five wins as the baseball season approached. Gary was leaving me alone at home and it was a welcomed silence because Duane and his buddies were not relinquishing their bullying.

During the end of track season, the captain and I were in full force. I had mastered Kenpo and within the first week of retraining, he presented to me the ways of handling weapons. Kenpo was an art I was coming close to mastering, but the weapons were a different story. The captain handed me two sticks, measuring fifteen inches each. They were of a thick wood and shaved and sanded to perfection. The feel was amazing, and he began showing me techniques to master their use. While training, their handling reminded me of a cheerleader holding batons and twirling them through the air. For over seven days, I would brutally experience pain like no other in my arms simply because these sticks were heavy. My forearms developed unwelcoming pain as I began controlling the movements of these weapons.

The symmetry involved in Kenpo gracefully turned me into a powerful machine and before I could blink, I was destroying the punching bag with ease. The quickness in my arms would work together and defeat the exercise the captain placed in front of me. The training controlled my breathing and the swagger of my movements excelled with each strike. I had excelled the mastery of Kenpo and now it was time to learn Taekwondo. I had always become interested in the art since I met Billy Blanks a year prior. Billy and his dojo had come to Masco to perform their moves and inspire others in the Boston area. It was an amazing show and I had always wanted to learn karate. Who hasn't seen the Karate Kid movies and wanted to be Daniel LaRusso? My answer was clear, and Billy Blanks piqued my interest. It would be later in life that Billy would end up a movie star and the mastermind behind the Tae-bo movement through the 1990's.

"Shawn, it's no secret Taekwondo is unique and can be executed in several different ways. This art form takes patience, good balance and I will teach you kicks at different heights, jump kicks, and spin kicks. I am going to show you all the different types of kicks. It starts with the front kick, and this sometimes is referred to as the snap kick because of the tremendous speed exerted in this move. It is one of the first kicks taught in Taekwondo but is often considered as one of the most powerful even at higher levels. It is performed by raising the knee of your kicking leg to the waist, then exerting force by exerting your foot forward, straight towards the target. This move is designed to push the target back, as well as injure them", he explained in full detail.

The demonstration was powerful, and I planted both feet in the grass of his front yard and practiced the front kick. I had very powerful legs and the snap was instant as if I was running over the hurdles. Upon practicing a few times, the captain was ready for the second demonstration.

"Another move is the side kick and this very powerful and has different implications depending on the style. It is performed by raising the knee while also rotating your body by 90 degrees,

then exerting force by extending your leg. By using the momentum of your waist and torso, you can connect harder with the target. Which part of the leg and foot connects with the target will vary between the different standards taught, but it will usually be with either the outside edge of your foot or with the heel of the foot. The roundhouse kick is a very powerful move. This kick is done by performing a pivot on the leg that is not kicking by turning your hips. While the pivot is conducted, contact is made with the target by extending your leg and impacting the target with either the ball of your foot or with the instep of the foot. Still with me?" He asked.

I nodded my head with the notion that he had a thousand percent of my concentration. The moves seemed much easier than anticipated and I spent the entire morning being his mirror.

"The back kick is more advanced, because as the name suggests, you would perform the kick by setting up for it away from the target. If it isn't done properly, you can easily lose the crucial balance to contact your opponent, or even fall over. The reverse

side kick is essentially an exaggerated version of the back kick. The difference is that this kick carries more power from the extra momentum, because the striker turns further than they would with the back kick. The Crescent kick comes in two variations: the inner and the outer. Both start off by raising your kicking leg as high against your body as possible and extending it, as well as placing it slightly across the centerline of your body. From there, if it is an outer kick, you will then sweep outwards from the centerline and connect with the target like this. If it is an inside kick, you would sweep towards the inside of the centerline, and connect with the target there. Does that make sense Shawn?" He asked.

"Yes, it does", I replied with a blank stare on my face.

This was a lot to take in and I was beginning to understand the differences of kenpo and taekwondo. It was imperative I understood the balance between defense and a quick offense. I was listening to his training, and it was superb.

"Now, the hook kick is a relatively modern trend, but is not common traditionally. It is like a roundhouse kick, but with a backwards sweep once the foot is extended. The intended impact on the opponent with this kick is meant to be the heel of the kicking foot. This is where your power will become crucial. Like the hook kick, this kick has a sweep performed to create an impact on the opponent. The difference here is that the sweep extends further, and the kick is performed with a perfectly straight leg. As with the hook kick, the heel connects with the target. The next kick is the Axe kick. To explain this complicated move, think of how you would swing an axe to cut a log. You first must lift the axe up above the height of your body, then the axe swings down onto the log, impacting it on a slight angle. The axe kick works by raising your leg up high towards the target, starting from outside the centerline. Once you have performed the upwards kick as high as possible, you exert downward force with this leg, and keeping the heel of the foot pointed downwards. The intended impact is basically everything above the torso of the opponent, including the head, shoulders, and collar bone", he fully explained.

I attempted all the kicks with fluid motion and the captain was impressed. I was a limber teen, and my new strength was pinned inside of my soul. The power was a work in progress, but the performance of the Kata, he trained me to initiate, worked with ease.

"Shawn, please understand these great points I am about to give you. Although not technically a kick, the knees are an essential part of any good kick, but they can also hold a lot of power on their own. The knee strike has many variations, but they all revolve around raising the knee and impacting the target by either bringing the target into the knee or pushing the knee towards the target. It involves hitting two opponents at once by performing a jump-kick and using each leg to target a separate opponent. It's a wonderfully impressive move, and one that you would surely be proud to master over time", he exclaimed.

Just as I thought everything was done, he surprised me with a last session.

"Are you ready to learn the last art I have for you?" He implied.

"*I am*", I replied with confidence.

"*Shawn, Aikido is a martial art that resembles methods of jujitsu and judo in its use of twisting and throwing techniques and in its aim of turning your attacker's strength and momentum against them. With this advantage, you can clearly defeat your opponent easily*", he stated.

For the next two days, the captain would teach me the basic techniques of Aikido so that I would be able to use my opponent's momentum against himself. I learned elbow and wrist controls and how I could easily apply pressure against an attack. I was easily learning how to take their momentum and using against them. It was a training that seemed to be particularly easy since I had mastered Kenpo. It was the equivalent of a batter standing inside of the batter's box and facing a 95 mile per hour fastball and simply turning the pitch inside out. It was a balance I was willing to perfect because Duane and the others were much taller than me. How come I didn't think of this before. They always travelled in pairs when they attacked me, but never alone. The techniques I was learning allowed me to focus on using their momentum against them and painfully applying pressure to force them to stop. I didn't need to defeat my opponent to show them my dominance, but rather stand my ground and become the wall they were unable to penetrate.

From several different types of strikes, to becoming the aggressor with a choke hold, I was now in full command. The lessons I had learned the past several months built me into a machine. Just as I had anticipated, the captain was a demonstrator to full capacity. His kicks were precise, crisp and very quick. I mimicked his moves to my best ability, but I had time to perfect the mistakes and terrible balance. While I admired his six-foot frame and two hundred pounds of solid muscle, my concentration was on his strong legs. He was built like a brick, and I was this scrawny kid who was slowly transforming into a much stronger boy. It's astounding to think it took a mysterious stranger to catapult my confidence through the stratosphere. I had learned the styles of Kenpo and Karate in the most important time of my life. I was proud of myself and felt very lucky to have the knowledge that I learned. The captain offered to bring me out to the mall for a huge surprise and celebrate my accomplishments.

The Saturday evening brought us to the confines of the Peabody Mall, and I had no idea what was in store. I knew the movie theatre was close by, but what was on this guy's mind? We ventured through the mall and decided to stop and eat some Chinese food and continued talking about my lessons. When he spoke, it was like reading a book that was interesting and you couldn't put it down. He was an excellent teacher physically and verbally, and he took me to the woodshed on self-defense. During the months of training, he would excel my body to heights I had never felt. During the evenings, the Charlie horses and cramps continued to ravage my muscles.

The strength within my body was felt within and I was garnering speed and accuracy. Those were my huge focuses on offense and the captain reminded me of my journey. I had not yet mastered each technique until I was able to exemplify control. That was the issue with most students in Karate because they used their tools as a weapon instead of a defense mechanism. If you watch the Karate Kid, you see what Daniel's focus and training all is about. A great defense is a good offense, and we learn that in life with sports as well. This was the key to my success in discipline and I had thought the captain disappeared into the bathroom, but his absence was excessive. I went to the bathroom, and I was greeted by two larger teenagers.

"*Hey punk! Give us your wallet*", one of the teens shouted.

I looked into the eyes of the overweight teen who still had pieces of his dinner stuck to his mouth. My assessment had him at barely taller than me and his little buddy was shorter than him. I was under the impression they had me mistaken for someone who cared, but they were relentless.

"*Hey asshole. Did you not hear me? I want your wallet*", the teen said again.

In the past, I would just run or get angry and begin yelling, but I felt a sense of calm. I was quick to react and reached in my pocket and grabbed my wallet.

"You mean this wallet", I stated while waving it slowly in the air.

I dropped the wallet to the ground and stood back in position, waiting for a moment. Just as the bully reached towards the ground, I grabbed the back of his shirt and lifted it over his head. His momentum brough him straight to the ground at my feet and his little friend began approaching me. While the large kid was unwinding himself from his shirt, little man lunged forward with a punch and missed my chest by inches. Hanging by a moment, I slid my body to the right and swiftly punched his inner bicep, limiting his strength in the middle of his swing. The hit was precise, quick and sharp as he pulled his arm back in agony. Grasping his arm, I jumped in the air and came hard down on his left knee with a down kick. The snapping of my foot created a brunt force and quickly buckled his leg. The little teen was now in pain in both his arm and leg, and I gave my attention to the larger asshole.

"Hey, I was paid a few bucks to harass you man. Please don't hurt me", he snarled.

"You boys have a nice night", I replied as I walked over towards the captain, who was waiting at the end of the hall.

"How much?" I smartly asked while leaning against the concrete wall.

"What do you mean?" He joked as we began walking towards the exit of the mall.

"Shawn, on a more serious note. I am leaving for Japan in the morning", the captain stated.

"I guess that explains tonight", I replied.

"You are ready my son. You have come a long way from the abuse you suffered from both your father and those boys?" He mentioned while driving home.

"Boys? How did you know?" I asked.

"Take what I am about to say very lightly and promise to control your anger like you did in the Mall back there?" He asked.

"I promise", I replied softly.

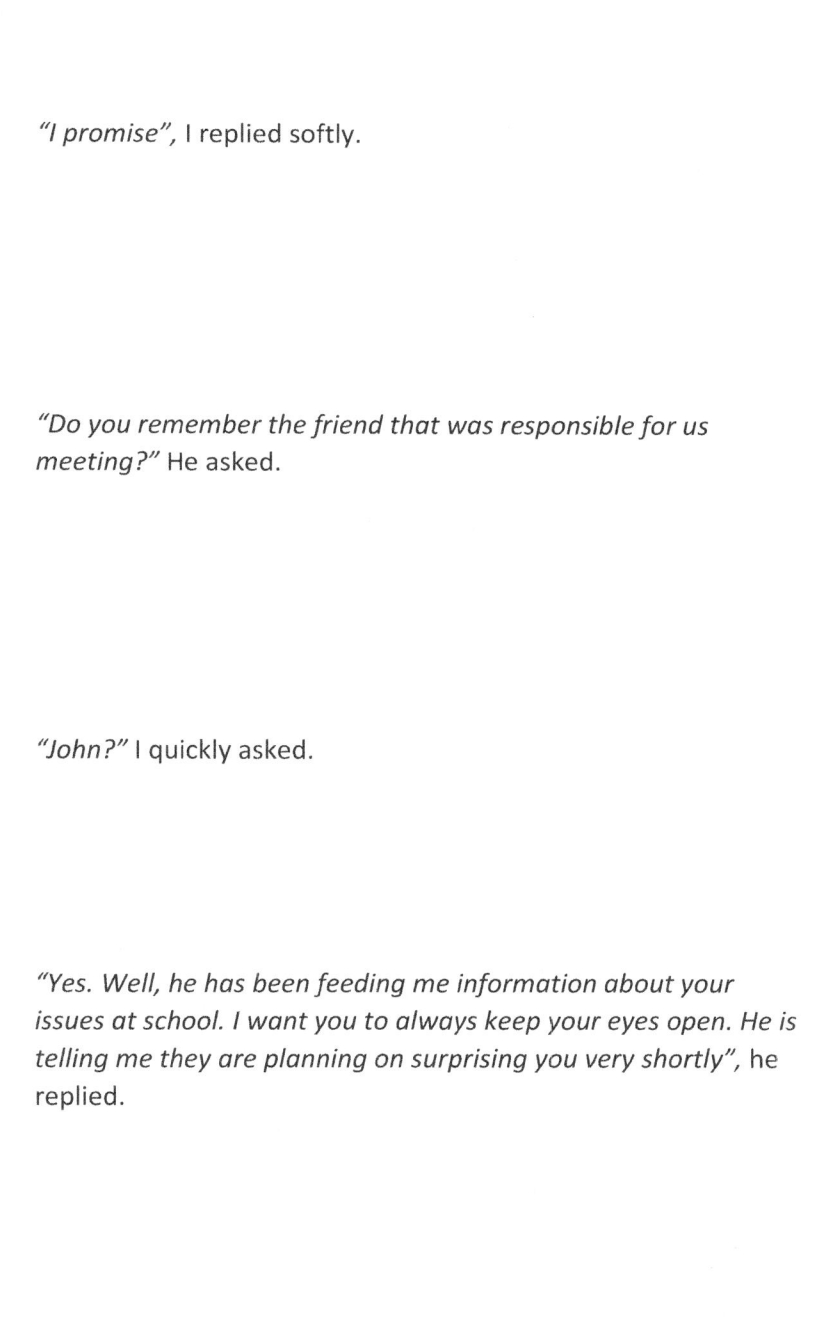

"Do you remember the friend that was responsible for us meeting?" He asked.

"John?" I quickly asked.

"Yes. Well, he has been feeding me information about your issues at school. I want you to always keep your eyes open. He is telling me they are planning on surprising you very shortly", he replied.

"I am ready", I replied with a quick smirk.

"I know you are, and I am proud of you Shawn. Thanks for giving me this opportunity to help you", he quoted.

The captain dropped me off at home that night and I spent countless hours running through the confines of the Nike Missile base and practicing kata on the walls of the abandoned buildings. I would run like a wild wolf and chase the demons that had attempted to puncture my heart.

I was preparing for the upcoming baseball season by working out every day in the gym during my lunch hour. The schedule stretched on for many days and since I was only one week away from tryouts, the treadmill called my name. The cold March precipitation kept me in the gym since I wasn't comfortable running in twelve inches of snow. While jogging, I glanced through the window of the hallway and noticed a classmate having issues at the door of the boy's locker room. His name was Andrew Washburn, and I could see his angst as he stumbled into the hallway. Wanting to check on him, I left the weight room and asked him if he needed help.

"Andy, is everything ok?" I asked.

"Shawn, I am ok. I don't think you should go in there. They are asking about you", Andrew stated.

"Who is asking about me?" I asked.

"We are you dick head. Why don't you and Andy come down and play?" The raspy voice asked through the open door to the boy's locker room.

Standing in the hallway, I looked down on the familiar voice to see Duane and his friend Craig staring up at me. This was my opportunity to instill my dominance upon the two boys who needed a lesson. These two dumb fucks were about to learn the hard way and it was going to be a nice, unexpected surprise.

Chapter 8
The Cult of Personality

The door to the boy's locker remained open as the invitation to join their party was indirect at best.

"Duane White. Are you and Craig jerking each other off in there and my friend Andy accidentally interrupt you?" I sarcastically asked.

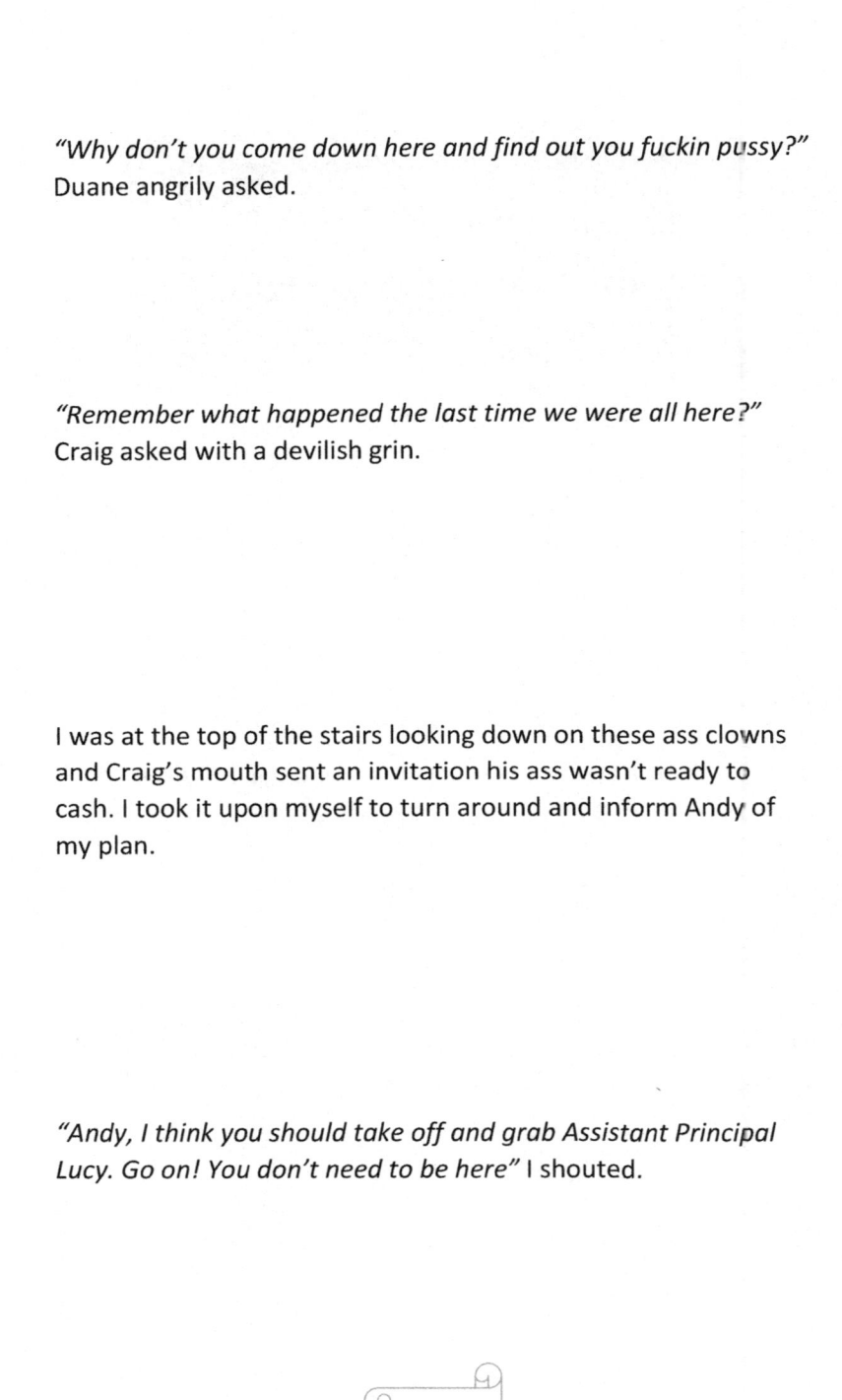

"Why don't you come down here and find out you fuckin pussy?" Duane angrily asked.

"Remember what happened the last time we were all here?" Craig asked with a devilish grin.

I was at the top of the stairs looking down on these ass clowns and Craig's mouth sent an invitation his ass wasn't ready to cash. I took it upon myself to turn around and inform Andy of my plan.

"Andy, I think you should take off and grab Assistant Principal Lucy. Go on! You don't need to be here" I shouted.

"Shawn, are you sure? I don't think you should go down there. They seem fucking drunk", Andy offered.

"Shhhhhhh!" I whispered silently with a finger over my lips as I closed the door behind myself.

Looking through the eyes of the two men who recently had raped me, I placed my right leg on the top step and casually walked to the floor of the locker room. I was locked in with focus and I remembered what the captain had taught me. Each step signifying the will to punish the men responsible for eluding my revenge. Both teens were tall, and I was destined to rip into their flesh, despite the height difference. Before the boys could say a word, I lunged forward and straight kicked Craig in his abdomen, knocking him to the ground. The speed was fierce, and Craig bumped his head harshly on the floor, leaving him in a daze. It was Duane and I alone for a moment and this was a piece of glory I deserved. He took his boxing stance and placed his right leg just behind his left. This was the avenue I needed for him to abruptly make a mistake and throw a punch. Just as I predicted, the punch came quick and inaccurately. The breeze was calm, but his strength eluded him. Duane appeared to be inebriated and this was far from a fair fight. Craig was on the ground wincing in pain, while his friend was shadow boxing and escaping his breath. I could see they were smokers and Duane was nearly out of breath after missing with a few punches.

"Are you going to tell me that you are already tired Duane?" I asked.

The look on his face was priceless because the anger and embarrassment surpassed him.

"I am going to kick your ass", Duane stated as he again lunged and missed with another punch.

It was all slow motion as his right hand passed the right side of my cheek, while I slid forward enough to face the side of his body. With one quick jab to the throat, Duane grabbed his neck and landed on one knee. Chocking uncontrollably, my nemesis took my knee to his head and fell to his back with a large forward thrust. I stood above him and looked down with an evil look of disgrace. The position of my legs could have easily ended his life with a stomp to his skull, but I hesitated. I wasn't fulfilled with what had transpired because I wanted Duane's full power. I deserved that chance and as I looked down upon his face, I opened my mouth.

"You and I are not done my friend. I will get what is coming to me and you won't take that from me. Am I clear? Clean yourself up", I stated while throwing a small towel at him.

I had picked him up by his shirt as he was choking for air. I released him to the floor and turned around towards the door of the locker room. I had enough of being bullied in this school and I had finally sent a clear message. I wasn't sure if I had awakened a sleeping giant or quieted the storm with my rhetoric. Either way, I felt free and continued my workout in the weight room. The commotion across the hall was silent and while the assistant principal investigated the incident, nothing would come of his reckless theories. Our magical assistant principal was something else and I spent many years avoiding the prick. Not one person liked him in our school and as I continued working out, I thought this was a beautiful day and as the week transpired, others in school took notice of my escape.

I grabbed my baseball mitt and I had waited all week to hit the baseball field. Varsity tryouts were here, and I was one of many in attendance looking to snag a roster spot for Masco's team. The baseball team had a history of decent teams, but never good enough to make the state playoffs. For us to climb the feat, our team would have to gather twelve wins in twenty games to qualify. Rick Anthony was the returning pitcher that was both dominant and had attracted a few pro scouts. He had an electrical fastball and a strong presence on the mound. Oh yeah, did I neglect to mention this is the same Rick I beat a summer ago in Babe Ruth?

Rick was a power pitcher and for Masco to succeed, they were attempting to rely on Kenneth Nazarian to be there number two. I had never seen his mechanics until today during tryouts and I was flabbergasted. If Masco's playoff chances relied on Ken to win five games, we were fucked. I contemplated skipping tryouts and qualifying for the junior varsity team, but I didn't have the patience. I was already expected to attend since everyone knew my reputation on the diamond. Coach Dick Sauchuk anticipated my arrival and without hesitation, I was throwing a few practice pitches from the mound. Since the previous summer, I hadn't thrown a baseball in a long while and my arm was strong. I couldn't believe how crisp the ball was releasing from my hand. The eyes of every potential player on the practice field paid close attention the loud pop from the catcher's glove.

Remember the man from the beginning of this story? His name is Jeff Milks, and he was the catcher of the varsity team. For the next couple of years, this teenager would be the focal point of my existence. Jeff was considered our best hitter and I had never seen him on the baseball field until now. When it came time to grab a bat and see everyone's strengths, he stood out next to home plate. He was merely a few inches under six foot, and he was built solid. He was a rat in the gym and his power was on full display with each swing of his bat. Everyone knew the junior was a huge talent and what they were expecting was a state playoff visit. If Jeff was to carry the team on his shoulders, it would take the guise of someone else to help. The player's list was compromised and full of many juniors. Coach Sauchuk had his work cut out for him and he would manage to build a roster of talented young men. I honestly didn't like the coach one bit, simply because he was a poor judgement of character. Many of the attendees were sent to the junior varsity and freshman teams, while some of us deployed our crafts on the varsity team.

Once tryouts were finished, our lineup was set, and it historically sucked. I was left off the batting roster because the coach didn't believe my assets were good enough. I could not fathom what made this idiot believe my near seven hundred batting average the past two summers didn't qualify for a starting spot. Looking at the order he created, there were seven or eight spots that called my name, but to no avail. Coach Dick Sauchuk left me off the roster because something was on his mind, and I always thought the players on my team had a lot to do with his decision. I was a cocky son of a bitch and maybe that rubbed people the wrong way. Rick Anthony was the lone person on the team that experienced my talent, yet he never spoke up for me.

Knowing what I had known, I took a long walk over the following weekend at the Nike Site to clear my head. I contemplated leaving the team and watch them fall apart miserably from afar. Masco's Varsity lineup was weak from the fifth position and beyond. If Dick was smart enough, he would have placed me in the five spot and put Ken Nazarian behind me. Kevin Winship was a perfect leadoff hitter with Jeff and Rick in the perfect three and four holes. After Ken, the lineup was a fucking wash, and it would take a miracle to get the bottom of the order to produce. Troy Anderson, Karl Klemm, and Mike Gillert were responsible for shoring the baseball order and I could never understand what Coach Sauchuk saw in them. I thought carefully at what I wanted out of this baseball team and all I could do is attempt to impress these fuckers with my arm. I was faster and stronger than I was the previous two summers, so I know what I was more than capable of.

The spring of 1989 saw the varsity baseball team gather their first state playoff visit in a long time. We had barely made it into the state bracket, and I contributed a solid five-win campaign in six starts. I started a third of Masco's games and as a team, we merely hit a shade over .260. The one game I lost was a one run defeat in the first game of the season against Marblehead, 2-1. They were considered a powerhouse of a team since they were in the same division as Salem High School, the eventual state champion. I had beaten Amesbury, Ipswich, Lawrence, Newburyport, and North Andover and never surrendered more than two runs all year. My earned run average was a hair below one and a half runs and when Dick Sauchuk was nice, he allowed me to garner nine at bats during my sophomore season. Despite getting four doubles and three singles, it did not earn his respect. I had just batted .778 during the season and he still thought it was necessary for me to ride the pine. Could our team perform better that we did? Yeah, sure. But it was all about Rick and his arm who had helped our team reach the state playoffs.

By the skin of our teeth, we tied for a wild card spot and needed a play-in win to make it into the State Tournament. Rick drew the assignment against Everett on our home field. Coach mentioned he would put me in the game if needed, because he wanted to win the game terribly. This was coach's chance and Rick didn't disappoint. Their pitcher was tough and upon surrendering three runs to our offense, his team would only muster two runs against Rick. We nearly blew the game when Karl Klemm had retrieved a fly ball in left field and when he threw it to home plate, he literally threw the fucking baseball in the woods. He was the weak link on our defense and offense, and I still can't understand how Dick started him over me all season. Despite the near catastrophe, Rick would finish his night with eight innings of five hit ball and two earned runs. Coach called on me to shut down the last three batters and not one was able to touch the ball. I struck out all three batters with fifteen pitches and Masconomet was proudly in the State Playoffs. Since our first game was five days away, coach asked me to start our official first game of these same playoffs.

The first round in the 1989 State baseball playoffs was against the confines of Jamaica Plain and their terrible demographic. Ever heard the name Whitey Bulger? Well, we were in his territory, and I had never heard of the guy in my life, but others were weary. The High School of Jamaica Plain was in a large stadium, surrounded by the confines of the Boston ghetto and its poor community. We were Masconomet and enshrined in the communities of the rich and powerful. We had Billy Joel and a lot of the players from the Red Sox in our community, so we were immediately shamed when a police escort brought us to the stadium.

"Good luck with these fuckers", Rick Anthony said on the bus as we saw the rowdy fans in their stadium.

What the players and students of Jamaica Plain didn't know about me was my inner exclusion. I had no idea what being rich and spoiled would be like, so when it came time to stand on their pitcher's mound, they collectively saw something of themselves. For seven amazing innings, I would strike out sixteen batters and surrender one run on three hits. It wasn't my best performance of the year but surrendering one unearned run didn't faze my confidence. Coach Sauchuk walked to the end of the bench and informed me I would be removed from the game. For the first time all season, I had enough of this guy's shit.

"Coach do not take me out of this game. I have two innings left", I shouted.

"Shawn, I might need you for the next couple of games. Let someone else take over, ok", he mentioned.

"What the hell coach. You have taken my offense away from me all year and now you are taking my defense? I have had enough of this. You take me out, I am done for good", I yelled in anger.

"I promise you will be a huge part of the offense next year. Please be patient and think of the team first", Dick mentioned.

Dick walked away and looked back at my frustration. He was solely responsible for handicapping our team with my bat remaining on the bench. I am confident to say we could have won seventeen to eighteen games this year if I had been placed in the lineup. The mediocre play of our bottom order and the horrible pitching from Ken Nazarian limited our ability to win more games. The disposition of our reluctance came from our crappy coach, and he made the decision to move forward.

Ken Nazarian would end up beating South Boston the following game 8-5, setting up a strong matchup against Stoneham. The talk of the town was Masconomet facing Salem, if we had surpassed this next game. I wanted Rick Anthony to finish strong, but he was relegated to a huge loss because his offense failed to support him. Our weakness caught up to our team and our baseball season was over. Stoneham would eventually lose their next game against Salem, while the juggernaut Salem team would claim a state title against Drury. These teams were filthy when it came to their pitching, and I solemnly wish coach had let me pitch against Stoneham. I would have easily shut them down for Rick to get his dream matchup against Salem.

Coach Sauchuk was a fucking dumb ass because the math was simple. Ken Nazarian hurt our pitching staff by combining with Rick Miranda to beat South Boston four days after the first-round win against Jamaica Plain. Rick Anthony was on five days rest when our second-round match against South Boston occurred. If Rick had pitched that game, it would have easily placed my turn in the rotation against Stoneham with five days' rest. Despite Stoneham beating Rick 4-1, I could have easily beaten that team with a shutout to advance our team against Salem. The Houston Astros first round pick was not set in the rotation to pitch the Regional Final, so Masco's chance to beat Salem was spectacular with Rick on four days' rest. If we would have supplanted Salem, I would have faced Middleboro in the State Semi-finals and allowed Rick to pitch against the powerhouse team of Drury and their all-state pitcher.

  The possibilities ran through my head, but if Dick had just put me in the daily lineup, I could have easily supplied our team with a lot of offensive opportunities as a sophomore. Let's remember, I played against a lot of these same players in the summer league, and I was a relentless machine in the batter's box. I was convinced fully in my mind if I was in the lineup for the entire 1989 season, I would have comprised an average near .600, and the past would have been written differently. The national player of the year for 1989 was Tyler Houston from Valley High in Las Vegas and be batted only .540, drafting second overall in the MLB draft.

How crazy would it have been to provide one of the best stats in the country on a miniscule division two team out of the town of Boxford, Massachusetts? Surrounding myself with the previous two summers, the freshman year prior and the seven hits out of eight at-bats this year, I easily can say I would have dominated and helped the team become better.

With only a few days left in school, I welcomed the summer with open arms. I considered my first season on the varsity team a huge failure. I could have been one of the best hitters in the entire country, but our coach was holding me back. I was beyond upset and I decided to enter the Bay State Games for the summer. The Bay State Games hosted a slew of summer sports for the teens of Massachusetts, and it had been around for many years. My next-door neighbor informed me of the massive invitation in the Salem Evening News and the attention I could receive from colleges and pro scouts was enticing. I was willing to give it a try and hope I could develop a reputation I was more than deserving to have and wake my baseball coach out of his coma.

The Topsfield Babe Ruth team was dominating over the first several games and I was angry. Each time I was on the mound or at the plate, I recalled the face of coach Sauchuk and I played with a sense of purpose. As a team, we collectively played perfect, and we didn't lose a game as the Bay State Games arrived. I wasn't prepared for the excitement the tournament brought the area and it was massive. Hundreds of baseball teens trying out for the many spots brought out competitive and exuberating of talents. I had only been involved with Masco baseball for a year, but players from Andover, Tewksbury, Salem, Hamilton-Wenham, Drury, and all over were present.

I was allotted ten pitches from the mound and several at-bats to showcase my talent, and I was chosen to play for the North team in our section. The coach of our team was from Salem, and he brought his own pitcher, Mike Giardi with him. I liked him right away and we bonded rapidly because we had a common goal here. We spoke about his Salem team and their state championship win. I recalled seeing Jeff Juden in the baseball stands of our last game and at six foot seven inches, how the hell could you not miss him. He was now a product of the Houston Astros and Mike was taking over the team in Salem. As we talked more and more the next couple of days, we became friends. He was interested in becoming a proud student-athlete at the University of Harvard and I was living my life hoping not to get killed by the man who called himself my father. I had explained to Mike the falling out with my coach at Masco and he just mentioned to be honest and talk with him. Mike had mentioned his father couldn't understand why I wasn't part of Masco's offense after watching my tryout at the plate. It was a huge compliment and a smart eye for talent, and Masco's Dick Sauchuk sucked at it.

This was a friendship I would cherish, but when it came to the games, our team played three in a row over the weekend. It was announced that Mike would start game one and I would start game two. College scouts and a few pro scouts were scattered throughout the stands on the Boston College campus. With a tremendous showing during several batting practices, I was assigned to start in right field and bat fifth in the lineup. We had an all-star lineup of future college prospects, and I was destined to make a name in this huge tournament.

Our first game began quickly in the morning, and Mike was in absolute control. It was hard to believe how deep the Salem High School roster was because Mike was considered their 3rd pitcher. He was in Ken Nazarian's spot, and he was a million times better. I would have given anything to have Mike on our team, but I was at bat in the bottom of the first with the bases loaded. The kid pitching to me was from South Boston and he had a weird stance. I was used to a pitcher with a wind up, but this young teen pitched from the stretch. He was quick with his momentum, but the calculations of his arm strength made no sense. His first pitch literally took a year to arrive at the plate and I watched it gracefully. Four of these slow pitches failed to touch the plate and I would be credited with an RBI and a walk. Several innings and many hits later, our team would win 16-1. I finished with two walks and three hits, and I was starved for more. We played back-to-back games on this Saturday, so before I could relax, I was on the mound throwing. I asked Mike's dad if I could still bat, but he was upfront in saying Mike and I would swap. This meant he was the DH, and I was in the pitcher's spot. It was a good decision because I needed all the strength I could muster. We had just played a three-hour game and we only had an hour to rest.

During the hour, I took time to reflect on the previous year and what I had put myself through. I was bullied to a point of no return and somehow, an angel in the form of a captain saved me. If it wasn't for him, my confidence would have suffered and since my near death in the front yard, Gary Wallis had kept his hands to himself. I was lucky to be alive and if the bullying had continued, I literally think I would have hung myself. I was raped by my uncle and these classless pieces of shit at school, and I felt as if I was trapped in my own prison. I was in a bad place for a very long time and today, I am starting one of the most important games of my career. I had forgotten how awful I was treated by my baseball coach and for a second, I was nearly perfect.

I was partaking in a game against the favored east squad. Earlier in the day, they mauled their opponent by ten runs and their lineup was loaded from top to bottom. This was the Bay State games and it felt more like a tryout for the major league farm system. Scouts were lined up behind the backstop and two radar guns sat atop their lonely tripods. The moment I stood atop the pitcher's mound, a nervousness gripped over me. I was used to pitching in big games over the last couple of years, but this was by far the biggest. My lucky number was twenty-one because of Roger Clemens, so I brought my uniform from the Babe Ruth league to wear. It was unique to see everyone wearing their summer uniforms and I had recognized a few from the opposing team. Topsfield was being represented on the mound and from the first pitch to the last pitch of the first inning, the mood was set immediately. I put myself into a gear I had never felt before, and my fastball became electric.

According to my coach, whispers through the crowd had my speed eclipsing 88-92mph. I had always thought my fastball was in the upper 80's, but today I was on another planet. Before each fastball, I literally threw as hard as I could, risking severe injury to my arm. I had never in my entire life thrown this hard, and the results were enormous. The noise from the large crowd lifted me onto a cloud high above the field. This was the biggest crowd and stadium I had ever pitched in, and I was showcasing myself for everyone to enjoy. Maybe I was selfish, but this was my one chance to wrap my name on the minds of the scouts. My changeup and curveball complimented my biggest pitch and through the first five innings, I had surrendered no hits. Despite the mood throughout the campus of Boston College, I had thrown nearly seventy pitches. I was on fire, and I didn't want to be removed from the game. Instead of replacing myself with a new pitcher, coach sat down next to me and put his arm around me.

"Today son, you pitched like Jeff Juden and you should be proud of that. The scouts here have seen enough to know that you are something special. You have nothing left to prove and I want you to save your arm for next year, because I will need you to help lead us. Besides, who else would I want facing me in the State Playoffs next year. Shawn, you should be proud of yourself here today. I promise I will give your coach a call and imply that

he put you in his lineup, because believe it or not, I think you are a better hitter than a pitcher. Please ice your arm and be ready to play tomorrow", he offered while placing his arm around me.

I had just thrown a no-hitter and the rest of my teammates congratulated me, knowing I had thrown my last pitch. This was one of the first coaches I had respected besides Coach Foreman of my summer league. He took the time to explain my removal, unlike Coach Sauchuk. There was something grazing my mind and I wish I had taken the time to remain open about my feelings. I wanted to leave Masconomet and transfer to Salem, but what would it take to accomplish that. I brought the idea to Mike, and he mentioned I would have to move to the Salem area. This was something I knew Gary Wallis would avoid because he wanted to foil my future than allow me to succeed. I knew if I could transfer to Salem, Mike and I would dominate the Northeastern League together and keep the state championship in Salem. For this to happen, I would need the one person's approval I knew was going to decline my request. Despite the blowout win, I collected another four hits at the plate of the third game against the west team. The bay state games resembled a tryout of sorts, but for who? There was no way Dick Sauchuk gave a shit about these results, but it was a springboard into the minds of the scouts. Could I possibly play for Salem next year, or succumb to another benched year at Masco?

When in doubt, I would always lean to the one person that was the softest in my life. My mother was a stay-at-home mom that put up with Gary and his alcoholism and physical abuse. It is not like Terri was innocent against my abuse because she never once tried to protect me. When I mentioned what Uncle Frank did to me back in 1981, she attempted to protect my assailant and pretend it never happened. She was more focused on the affair with her husband's nephew than me, and I can only assume she did the same for my sister when her husband's father sexually assaulted her daughter. What type of parent's were these two idiots? I asked that question every day of my entire life and I needed my mother to come through for me. She owed this to me because I could garner more attention on Salem's roster as an All-American junior in pitching and hitting. God damn it she owed me, and I was numb to the fact she could convince her husband to think of my future.

It was a hot summer day, and my junior year was a couple of months away. I was on the verge of driving myself crazy, so I suddenly spoke to my mother. I had mentioned that I wanted to transfer schools and just as I began, I was shut down quickly.

"Shawn, have you lost your mind? Your father went through a lot to get us here and we just can't leave on a whim. I am sorry, but you are going to have to suck it up and deal. There is no way we can afford the housing", she replied rudely.

I called Mike Giardi and told him the bad news. He was a bit frustrated with me, but we wished each other luck and I would not see him again until next year. This was the summer of 1989 and I had decided to work hard and get my career to move forward in baseball. It was Mike Lindquist that told me in the middle of a game that coach Bouvier had been removed from Masco. The new coach was a teacher at the school, and he was given a chance to break the curse at our high school. Our football team had been bad for so many years, we were included on an ESPN episode back in 1988 as one of the worst teams in the entire country. How awesome is that? We were recognized nationally when Ipswich High School came to town that same year, as the running back set a state record that put him on ESPN. It was Bouvier's crappy defensive scheme that put him in the spotlight, but for negative reasons. Somehow and someway I always imagined Coach Bouvier was proud of that moment. He had done something to attract attention to our program, but he had to go.

Since I had retired from football, Mike had asked if I could come back to the team. His explanation was in the third person because it was Jeff Milks and Mike Gillert that wanted me back. They had apparently been elected team captains ahead of the season, so it was at their bequest to get me back. For this to occur, I would have to commit to the double sessions for the program and I was ready. I was in the best shape I had ever been and coming off a championship at the Bay State Games and Summer league, football was now in full swing. I hadn't lost a game all summer and sharing the most valuable player award with Mike Giardi was impressive at the Bay State Games. I had put myself out there and as a junior now, a lot of focus was centered on my play. I didn't know how much I could offer the football team since Jeff was named the starting quarterback. He was in desperate need of a number one wide receiver, so I elected to fulfill the position. Mike Gillert and I would succumb to the demands of Coach Pugh. He was the new coach of our football team, and he was dedicated immediately. His impact would effectively take a while to catch on, but I was proud to be a part of a new movement at Masco.

I knew our football team was in over their heads because we were considered the doormats of the Cape Ann League for a long time. What the rest of the league did not know, was our new offense would propel ourselves to be free of the Bouvier system that had failed for years.

The summer sessions were tough, and Coach Pugh was determined to see us suffer. I never took it personal, but the misery of the heat put a bond between our team because we didn't want to lose anymore. The new offense took time to learn, but I was impressed with the route tree that coach implemented into the playbook. Numbered one through nine, the routes each receiver ran depended on the number called in the huddle. I was considered one of the fastest players on the team, so of course I wanted to always run a long post or a fly pattern. Coach Pugh loved to call my number and he worked me to death late in the hot summer. Whether it was a jet sweep or a screen pass, I was the center of attention for his new quarterback. I was very weary of our offensive line because we didn't have the muscle or weight to sustain drives. Jeff was tough and he had a much better arm that I anticipated. He was a great athlete, and it was the football team that brought us closer together. I never felt that Jeff and I were great friends, because I always considered him an older brother.

He was my catcher the previous year and we bonded just enough to understand that winning meant everything. I just couldn't understand why he didn't want me in the lineup last year. What did he not like about me? Did he not comprehend my talents at the plate? Would he have been upset if I had attracted all the attention and he was relegated to being second? I feared that was the issue and I kept my distance with Jeff personally. What he didn't understand was the attention our baseball team could have received nationally. If I was to supplant our offense into a powerhouse, everyone on the team would have received attention. Jeff really missed out on a golden opportunity to push for my position in the lineup.

I wanted to be perfect for Jeff and since he was the leader of our team, I made it a focal point to be his crutch. Before the school year began, a scrimmage with a team from New Hampshire would clearly define where we were as a team. Coach Pugh's brother brought his High School team down for a friendly scrimmage and he warned us of their size. Once their bus arrived, we wondered why each player had issues seeing over their own seats. All jokes aside, this team from out of the area was quick, fast and ready to play. It was agreed to play an entire half of football, while every player was evaluated. Despite my height difference with their cornerbacks, their speed and aggressive play made it hard to break off the line. Our offense struggled mightily and through the first quarter, we managed just a few first downs. We were only down a touchdown as our defense tightened up as the strength of our team. I was responsible for covering their best wide receiver and it would eventually come to fruition that their running game was superior. They garnered over a hundred yards in the first quarter on the ground, but they failed to complete one pass.

The second quarter was a different story and Jeff was able to connect on several passes. Both drives resulted in touchdowns and our swagger could not be any better. Our team's confidence was rising, and our defense made a few crucial mistakes and allowed the final fourteen points, resulting in the seven-point defeat. For the first time, I never thought a loss could teach us more about ourselves than this one. We worked together once adjustments were made, and our confidence was high heading into our first game of the 1989 season.

Coach Pugh had his work cut out for him, but we were not an overconfident team. We were the same team that got abused the last few years, but there was one huge difference. We had a new system we believed in and that was a starting point any team could live up to. I thought the summer was successful and I was looking forward to attending my first day at school as a junior. I didn't think much would be different, but I was far from wrong. My friends Travis Larrabee and Andrew foreman literally grew overnight. I was witnessing our friends and classmates growing before our very eyes. Puberty was in full force and so were the bullies that I despised. On the first day of school, Duane and his friends Jody and Craig made themselves known. Walking by my locker, Duane stopped and mentioned he didn't forget what happened and that I was dead.

I could care less what he said, and I could have easily embarrassed him in front of my class, but I wanted no part of it. I wasn't going to sit and allow this dipshit to ruin my year, but I knew I had to figure something out. This was going to be a great year and I had plans for Duane, but I needed to be patient. Really patient!

Chapter 9
Indemnification

The football season was beginning, and it didn't start off like we wanted. All the confidence in the world didn't prepare our team for Bishop Fenwick. With great anticipation, we performed in front of a packed house against our archrivals. I had beaten them twice in baseball and track, but we sucked something awful when it came to football. Despite the decent eighty yard receiving day, our offense was unable to get anything going as we were blanked 29-0. It was a valiant effort by our team, but the surprising news came from coach that I was to quarterback the junior varsity.

"Shawn, can I speak with you in my office?", Coach Pugh asked through his office door.

I was in the middle of getting dressed in the locker room and without warning, coach needed to meet me. Not sure why, but I didn't hesitate. I walked up to his office and closed his door behind me.

"What's up Coach?" I asked.

"Shawn, nice game today. I was very impressed with your defense. I would like you to give the receiver just a little more room. Those two flags today hurt our chances of stopping them on third down", he explained.

"Yes sir. No excuse for the flag on my part, was playing aggressive", I replied.

"Trust me, I know. Love the hunger you gave us. How are you feeling?" He asked.

"I feel good Coach. I am sorry about giving up those plays", I explained.

"Water under the bridge now. Shawn, the reason I called you in here was to inform you of your position with the junior varsity team. I need you to learn this offense and what better way than to run it on my JV team. You will need to wear #7 for the games. Are you ready to show me what you can do, because I know what you are capable of", he stated.

"I would really like that. When is our first game?" I asked.

"Monday afternoon", he stated.

I didn't have much time to learn the position, so as I had walked out into the locker room, Jeff was waiting.

"So, you need to learn the offense as a quarterback now, correct?" He asked with sarcasm.

"Yeah. Something about taking over as the new QB of the team", I responded jokingly.

Jeff laughed it off and agreed to help me. I figured he was being helpful because coach insisted.

"Shawn, how about I pick you up tomorrow and we go over this here tomorrow at the field?" He asked.

"You can count us in too", Mike Gillert responded as he approached.

"Great news. Pick me up at the Nike site. Know where that is?" I asked.

"Yeah, that is where Mike lost his virginity with his sister", Jeff joked.

Jeff, Mike and I would spend hours going over the plays and for them, there was no investment here. I was glad they offered the help and as Monday approached; the school day couldn't get by fast enough. I was more than ready to lead the JV team against Bishop Fenwick. I was expecting a tough team to come onto our home field and really give us a test. Unfortunately, Rich Crosson, Mike Lindquist and many of the guys manhandled the front line of their defense. We scored four touchdowns in the first quarter in route to a huge 49-7 whooping. I was unaware of the school record, but I had thrown six touchdowns and lead the same team I had in the previous years. If you recall, this was merely the same team I had during my freshman year, and we were dominant. No question I had mastered the offense and with the next few weeks passing quickly, we had accumulated a record of 3-1.

The Varsity team was amid a four-game losing streak to start the season. We were aware the team was in a rebuild, but it was the seniors I felt bad for. Losses by Cape Ann league teams Pentucket, Amesbury and Hamilton-Wenham prevented our team from aspiring for the goal of a .500 record. It would take a miracle to improve the offense, since we were averaging 3.5 points per game. We surrendered a blistering 27 points per game and there was no stopping the bleeding. The next game was the pitfall of our season as we had lost 38-0 to an equally horrible Ipswich team. If there was a team, we all had hoped to beat, it was this team. Our JV team would move forward to win their five games and remain once beaten.

The rumor going around was Jeff would be replaced as QB of our team. I didn't quite agree with the decision because he wasn't to blame. Poor line play was mostly the problem and Jeff ran for his life each game. I wanted to do something, so I took the initiative to announce a surprise, like I had done before as a freshman.

"Coach, can we talk for a few minutes", I asked as I knocked on his door.

"Shawn, what can I do for you son?" He asked.

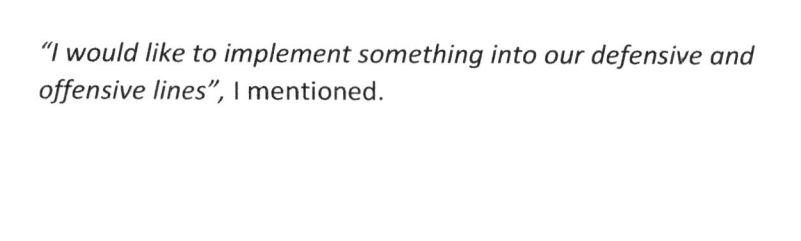

"I would like to implement something into our defensive and offensive lines", I mentioned.

"What did you have in mind?" He asked politely.

"We are getting our butts kicked out there and I would like to swap a few of the guys around and implement more blitzing. This man-to-man defense we are running is exposing our one-to-one matchups on the defensive line. If we could shore up the 34 defense and bring in the safety a lot more, we can be more successful against the run and the pass", I mentioned without hesitation while drawing the x's and o's on the chalkboard.

"*Shawn, thanks for the advice and I will take it under advisement*", coach stated while turning around and asked me to let myself out.

I had no idea if what I said upset him, but I wouldn't find out until Friday night against Newburyport.

When we arrived at the stadium in Newburyport on a Friday evening, we all sat in the locker room in silence and coach had informed our team of the new changes. We were shaking things up on defense and running a more effective blitz scheme. I had no idea how effective it would be, but I was onto something. The look on the players faces changed their identity and though process. For the life of me, I truly think they were in awe of my ability to help change the coach's mind. Looking back at coach throughout the game, he finally nodded his acceptance of my advice. We were in a dogfight and Jeff looked better than he had in weeks with more room in the backfield. We eclipsed over

100 yards rushing for the first time all year and despite our glory, we fell short 14-0. Psychologically, we had a win in our minds, and it was a moral victory in many ways. We had a new scheme and coach implemented it into the offense the rest of the year. It was the conversation the next day that would change my opinion for the rest of my life about him.

"Shawn, I want you to start this Saturday against Triton. If I recall, you beat them the last two years by a combined score of 61-10. Are you up for the challenge?" He asked in silence.

You would have to be a fly on the wall to hear my heartbeat after his question. I swear you could hear the paint peel off the concrete walls, and the pressure started to mount. I was not in position to dethrone Jeff because he was my friend. Despite his reluctance to help me garner a position in the lineup for our baseball team, all I could think about was his dedication to make sure I was ready to take the reins in 1991. I wasn't prepared to do that to Jeff, so I calmly declined without remorse.

The look on coach Pugh's face was pure anger and without hesitation, he ordered me out of his office and his team. Let me repeat this for the entire world to hear. This man just kicked me off his team for basically sticking up for one of his struggling players. It was Jeff who needed to work out his issues, not me. Could I have taken the reigns and did a lot better? Yeah, maybe. It wasn't my moment to dictate, and I gladly accepted the ass chewing. Even when thirty years would pass ahead, Jeff Milks and the others never knew why I left the team. I was sticking up for what I believed, and he was our leader, and I wasn't taking that from him. Eventually the defensive and offensive schemes would allow Masco to win their first game by one single point.

Despite seeing it from afar, I was Jeff's biggest fan, and I was glad they could pull out their first victory in years. The junior varsity missed my presence and would lose the remaining four games with ugly losses. Whenever someone asks you what the most important position on a team is. Respond with this answer: Quarterback.

Dan Marino and Joe Montana were the largest reasons the Dolphins and 49'ers were always near the top of the standings. The Masconomet Chieftains football team of 1989 were a glorious, spontaneous and wild bunch of guys that played with a freedom unseen in years. Coach Pugh was secretly building a dynasty and I will always take credit for the new defensive schemes he implemented that year and beyond. Could we have won our final four games with me at the helm that year? Who knows, but it was Jeff's moment, and I wasn't at liberty to steal it from him and the guys. I was proud of their accomplishments and if leaving the team was best for me and Jeff, then so be it. I want to you hear this Jeffrey Milks from me. I was never going to allow my pride to get in the way of your season and I will forever know it was the correct decision to walk away. The team was yours to lead, whether you stood or fell with grace. I was enabling the chance to sit back and watch Jeff have the moment he needed, but at what price? Despite my actions, I was never thanked nor was my batting skills ever introduced to our team with Jeff's recommendation.

I was now on the prowl and with only a month before track season, I decided to befriend someone with the goal of revenge on my mind. The plan I had pursued in my head was coming to a head, and it was time to pick the perfect person to help with my revenge.

Her name was Jessica Dimond and she and I had known each other since my inception into eighth grade. She and I had never really gotten to know one another, but I took it upon myself to reach out. I called her home after getting her number from a mutual friend and the rest is history. She had always liked me over the years and when she heard my voice, she was under the impression I would be asking her on a date. Why do I know that? Well, she was blunt as blunt could be and I agreed to ask her out. I was intending on befriending her the best to my ability and the real reason for her becoming my girlfriend was no secret. That will come later.

Jessica and I had nothing in common and she convinced me to get dressed as she drove over to my home and picked me up for our date. Talk about a fast mover on my part. She was relentless, impatient, and spontaneous, and I liked it. We went out to the town of Danvers and settled in for a nice dinner of her choosing. My mother was nice enough to hand me over some cash so I wouldn't completely embarrass myself and become a gentleman. She was a bit on the Metallica side of life with the dark hair, dark makeup, red lips and tight jeans. I wasn't very attracted to her appearance, but I was interested in her friendship with a girl named Christina Dellea. During dinner, we spoke about life, school and yes, her friend Christina. They had been friends for a long time and the reason I was interested would shock everyone. I had an issue with her boyfriend and his name was Duane White. My ploy was at the very beginning stages and Jessica was now front and center of my indemnification.

The evening wound down and Jessica and I ended the night locked in an hour's long kiss in her car. She drove a small four door sedan owned by her parents and they lived in the adjacent town of Middleton. Jessica was a good person and I wanted nothing to do with her inside of school, so I politely asked that we keep things quiet. After this long night, she would understand my issue with Duane and his friends and abided by our agreement. We would secretly see each other during the winter and keep things on the down low. This was the opportunity and angle I had been waiting for and Jessica was indirectly going to be my liaison to Duane.

I invited Jessica inside and my mother immediately took a liking to her. Upon staying for a moment, Jess drove the car home and offered an enticing invitation. When I had went to bed that evening, I sat up and thought about another plot I needed in my life. Jessica wanted to spend the entire weekend with me and since it was Friday, I invited her over the next day and my parents didn't care. They liked Jessica and she was welcome to stay all weekend since her parents were not going to be home. Before us talking, the plan was for Jessica to stay with a friend near her home. My parents trusted us to a certain degree, so Jessica and I cuddled in my bed for the evening without question. Before anyone gets a naughty thought in your head, please understand the circumstances here. Jessica was a gorgeous young woman, and I had this girl with a near perfect body laying against me, and I had to keep my hands to myself. Believe it or not, Jessica was a good girl, and I was hopeful for that. Despite the kissing, we were behaving and since the attraction was slight, this was a good thing, because I had plans for something sinister the next day.

"Jessica are you up for a long road trip tomorrow. I have something I need to do, and I am asking you to help drive me there", I whispered in her ear.

"Are we going to get in trouble?" She asked with a huge smile on her face.

"More than likely", I stated with a giggle.

"Count me in Mister Wallis", she replied.

We closed our eyes, and it was a long night. It had been ten years or more since I slept beside a girl. It was weird and exciting wrapped in one and her breathing against my chest kept me warm. The temperature outside reached well below twenty degrees and the heat from her body electrified my heart. Here this stranger was lying beside me, and I didn't deserve her beauty. Afraid I would fall asleep and snore, I slightly turned on my side on the single mattress and I let her spoon me. The adventure that lies ahead was deserving and clueless. I had no idea what I was in for, but I needed Jessica's help and she needed to remain naïve towards the plan I was implementing. This was something that took years to conjure, and she was the last piece of the puzzle to put things into perspective. The sound of peddling snowflakes tapped the window next to my bed and I slowly fell asleep.

We had woken up late that morning with huge smiles and kisses. This girl couldn't stop kissing me and she was driving me insane. She was amazing and when it came time to get dressed and eat breakfast, I took the time to cook her one amazing meal. She was unaware of my true feelings, and I didn't ever want Jess to understand her real meaning in my life. She was the bridge between two revenges and, I had a feeling she would slither away and relinquish her feelings once the plan was in place. There was no doubt Jessica liked me and I couldn't understand why she never wanted me around before. Maybe she was shy or thought I was too busy, but regardless, we were here. We got into her car and began driving south in the light snowfall. We took Interstate 95 south and drove around the city of Boston.

Jessica was not a talker, and the silent awkwardness gave way to the strangest question.

"Why did you wait this long to ask me out?" She asked.

"I am calling bullshit here. You didn't realize how I would give you a lot of attention back in eighth grade when you first met me?" Jess asked.

"Jessica. There is a lot you don't know about me, and I don't think you would have liked me after I told you. I moved here because I had no option", I replied with a sad face.

"When Cheryl introduced us back then, there was just something about you I loved. Remember that movie, 'Over the Edge'? You know, the one with Matt Dillon as a rebel and he befriends this stranger from out of town", she mentioned.

"I just watched that movie last weekend. Great movie", I replied.

"Shawn. The stranger in that movie has always reminded me of you. Just wish you had come after me years ago", she stated.

"I get that Jess, I do. I have been through so much over the years with my abusive Father and these fucking bullies", I accidentally mentioned.

"Bullies? What bullies Shawn. What are you talking about?" She desperately asked.

I attempted to cause a distraction by directing her to route three on our way to the town of Weymouth. She had no idea where we were going, but Jessica had a point. I was using this beautiful person to get something that had escaped me for years. There was no reason for her to comprehend the notion of my plan, so she remained silent and drove the car to where I had asked. After the long hour's drive, we pulled into the parking lot of my old Junior High School. I was there to meet someone and without provocation, my plan was forming into shape.

Her name was Sharon Verney and I had never lost contact with my old friend from eighth grade. She was the one source of information these past few years and we kept it a secret for years. We spoke once a month and she promised to keep tabs on the boys who had nearly killed me in the woods. She was the only friend from junior high that called to check about me after the beatings. Sharon was an angel and she agreed to always help me when I needed it.

"Nice to you see you Shawn", Sharon greeted with a huge hug.

"Nice to see you too. Has anyone begun showing for this bonfire?" I asked.

The bitter cold had brightened both our noses and the chilling of her bones was obvious. The temperature was dropping quickly while snowflakes fell softly on the ground. The plan was evolving into fruition and the night would open my invitation. Traditionally, the old class from junior high would gather to honor the fight that occurred on this same day three years earlier. Sharon and I had planned this for two years together and it was the time I needed to get my revenge.

We briefly spoke for a few moments, and I needed her to understand my position and no better person could get me. Sharon was a good person, and she took the time to secretly help me get to this point.

"Thank you, Sharon. I got this from here. I recommend you go home and stay there. Whatever happens, you never knew I was here. Do you understand?" I directed with a question.

"Shawn, no matter what happens. Always remain in control. I love you my friend and be careful", she responded with a huge hug.

Watching Sharon walk away, the remanence of the horrible night a few years earlier engraved hatred into my eyes. I stared off into the distance as the sky proclaimed a portrait of misery and revenge. Tonight, was my night and I had patiently waited this long for it, and I was delighted for its conclusion.

Chapter 10
Night of the Hunter

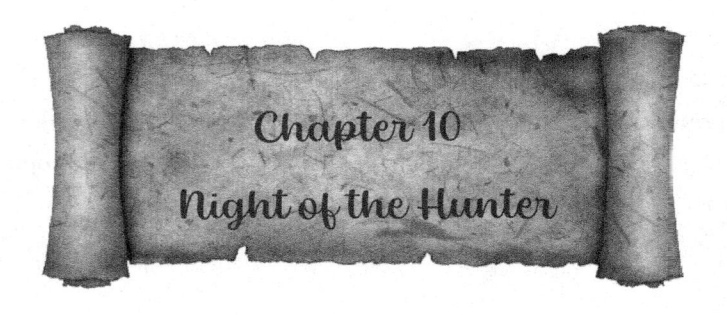

Darkness was a few hours away and instead of sitting in the car and freezing our asses off, we decided to visit a local restaurant. Jessica didn't ask any questions and it was hard to comprehend. Did she really care about me or was she up to her own plan? I had to keep my enemies close at some point in life and this was no different. I was succumbing to the visions of a hunter going after his prey and this was my cold dish. I was focused beyond any comprehension I had ever become a part of, and time was not a friend to my enemies. As we sat for a late lunch, Jessica couldn't help noticing I had brought a large sports bag. She was quiet until now, and her inquisition began. Jess had this nervous twitch about her as she chewed the inside of her lip and shook both knees under the table. I had reached across and grabbed her hand and gently looked into her eyes. No words were needed because my eyes spoke to her with kindness, and she became easily lost.

Here she was, over an hour away from home with a perfect stranger and thinking he was going to rob or kill someone. The anticipation was keen to her anxiety, and it bolstered a level of curiosity, exciting her. Looking down on the hand holding her, she began to speak.

"Shawn, why are we here in Weymouth?" She asked.

"*I want you to ask me that question tomorrow, ok?"* I replied with a question.

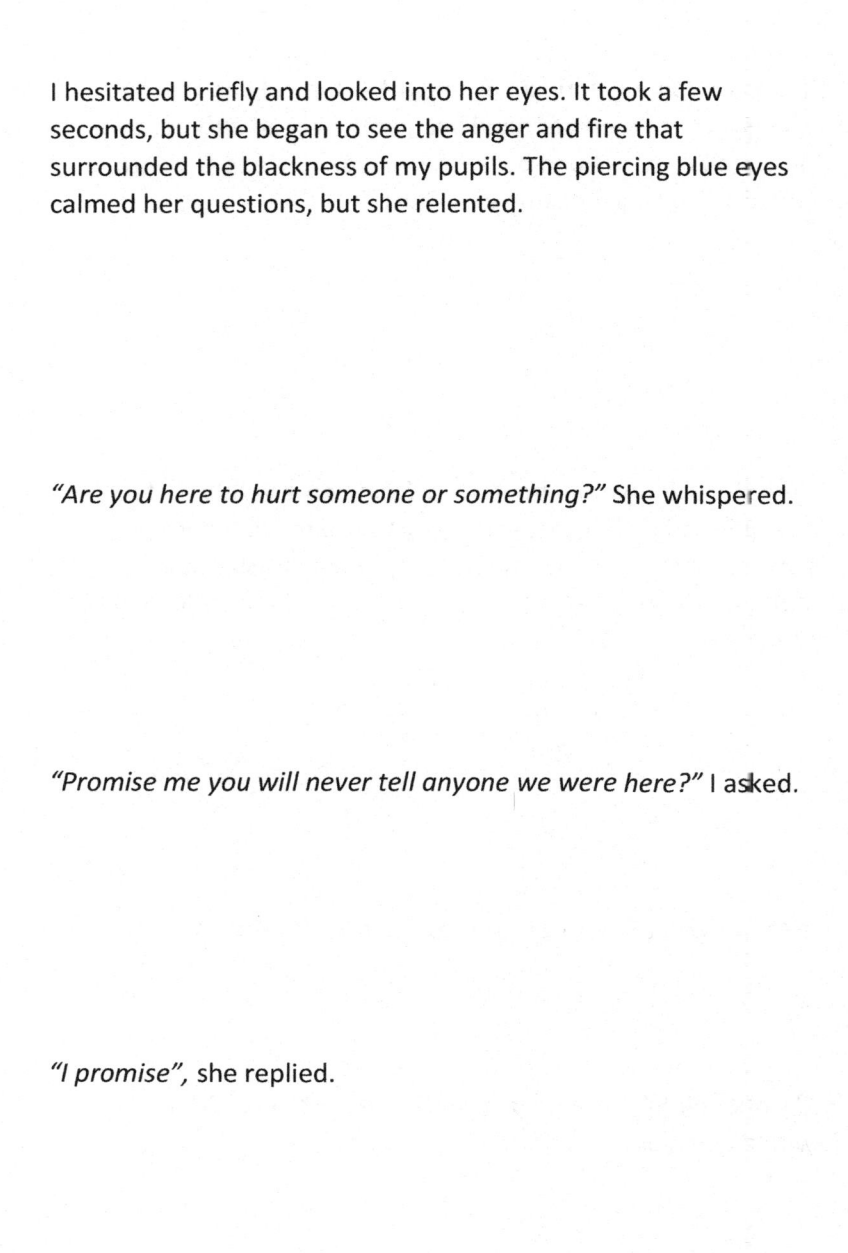

I hesitated briefly and looked into her eyes. It took a few seconds, but she began to see the anger and fire that surrounded the blackness of my pupils. The piercing blue eyes calmed her questions, but she relented.

"Are you here to hurt someone or something?" She whispered.

"Promise me you will never tell anyone we were here?" I asked.

"I promise", she replied.

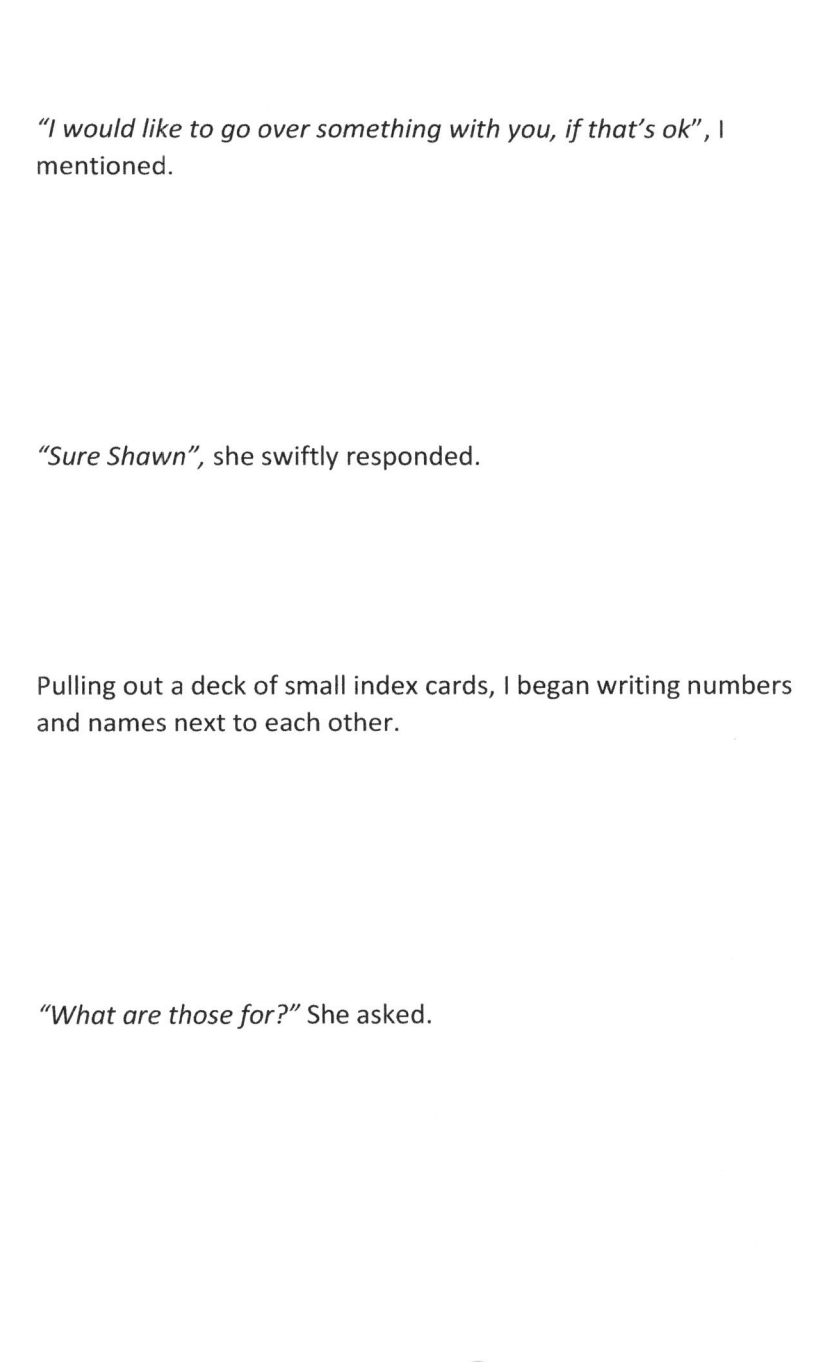

"I would like to go over something with you, if that's ok", I mentioned.

"Sure Shawn", she swiftly responded.

Pulling out a deck of small index cards, I began writing numbers and names next to each other.

"What are those for?" She asked.

"Jessica. I have a very important meeting with Principal Smith on Monday morning. These cards are a simple distraction away from today's purpose. Whatever you hear over the next week at school, let it go out of your ear and please do not repeat anything of it to your friends or anyone", I mentioned.

"Oh. This sounds interesting Shawn. Anything you want to share now?" She asked.

"I will when the time comes. In the meantime, please disregard anything you hear about me", I stated.

I used a pen and began writing names and numbers on each card. If you were a stranger with strange eyes, you wouldn't begin to understand the complexity of the information. I was labeling each card with a name, style of karate, and number. They would be complacent of rank for each card, and they were going to be implemented into my plan. Jessica watched me fill out fifty cards with false information for a period of a couple of hours.

I had a plan in place congruent to my position here in South Weymouth. It would involve a lot of thinking, preparation and one dumb girl to fall for my charm. Jessica was the perfect specimen, and the timing couldn't have been any better. Each night after training with the captain, I would calmly devise a scheme to plan the perfect scenario. Tonight, is a special night that would culminate in the beginning of my revenge, and it was to supplant all the bullies in my life. I was beyond prepared and if tonight goes as planned, it would help springboard everything else like dominoes falling perfectly. Synchrony was important and in a span of a year, the schedule was slowly coming to light and Jess helped expedite it by a year.

I was on a mission and the blank stare on my face placed focus on the task in front of me. The teens responsible for my near demise didn't receive the punishment they deserved, and I was the punisher. This was my night for the taking and as we finished our late lunch, the falling snow began blocking visibility. It was hard to determine the time without looking at our watches since it was beginning to darken. The afternoon in Boston would help blanket the light of the sky and darkness fell earlier than expected.

"Jessica. I brought you here for a reason and I want you to stay in your car with it running. We are going back to the Junior High School, and I have something I need to do", I responded.

"I won't ask you what you are up to, but will you promise to tell me when we get home later?" She asked.

We got into the car and drove back towards our destination. The roads were covered in salt and the melting snow softened my conscience. The visions of my beating kept flashing before my eyes, and I wanted to hurt these guys with all my heart. While Jess was at the wheel, I climbed into the backseat and opened the large black bag. I pulled out a pair of dark shoes, black shirt, dark colored wind breaker, and a brown ski mask. Jessica's eyes looked in the rear-view mirror and I could only imagine what she thought. She was probably thinking I was going to rob someone, but a huge part of my heart knew better. She was left to whisk in the dark and just as we arrived, I was in full gear. Jessica took one look in her rearview mirror and captured a horrific glimpse of something evil and unforgiving. I opened the rear car door and stepped out into the cold.

"I need you to stay here with the car running. If I am not back in thirty minutes, drive home", I directed as I leaned down to kiss her warm lips while lifting the mask over my mouth.

"Please hurry back and be safe. Whatever you plan on doing Shawn, I hope this is what you really want", she mentioned.

Equipped with two wooden short sticks given to me by the captain, the black cloak surrounding my body kept me blended within the darkness of the parking lot. The falling snow was relentless, but it was clear to see the footprints leading to my destination were slowing eroding. Unaware of what lie ahead, Sharon warned me of the potential dangers and the amount of people in attendance. Over the years, she always updated me with pictures of my assailants and their activities. The reconnaissance was merely important because today I was seeking my revenge. This is what I had prepared for, and nothing was going to prevent this night from becoming history. I had easily taken the pictures from Sharon and memorized the boys growing up over the years. Their faces were etched in my brain and my anger slowly subsided enough to seek their lives.

I grabbed the spray paint can from the inside of my jacket and began painting a message upon the walls of the Junior High. I was in full focus and my anger spread themselves upon the walls of regret. Unaware of the message it was to bring many decades later, I couldn't relent. These were the words from my heart bleeding on the pages of reality. I was a sixteen-year-old teenager attempting to right my wrongs and I was declaring war on my bullies. I may have been a maggot to them, but my pulse was bleeding red and the words upon my mind swiftly represented my vengeance.

This declaration was a reminder to those who dare cross their lines into the darkness of a stranger. I was offering a permanent solace against the bullying of anyone willing to offer a friendly hand in being kind and rewarding. The rage inside my soul followed my hands of unrelenting focus and the few sentences garnered my message. Upon finishing my scripture, I stood back in the falling snow and prepared to fixate upon the necessary evil.

It was my masterpiece, and it was located under a large lamp post near the same cafeteria I had gathered before walking into my beating. Like a ninja in the night, I took the same path I

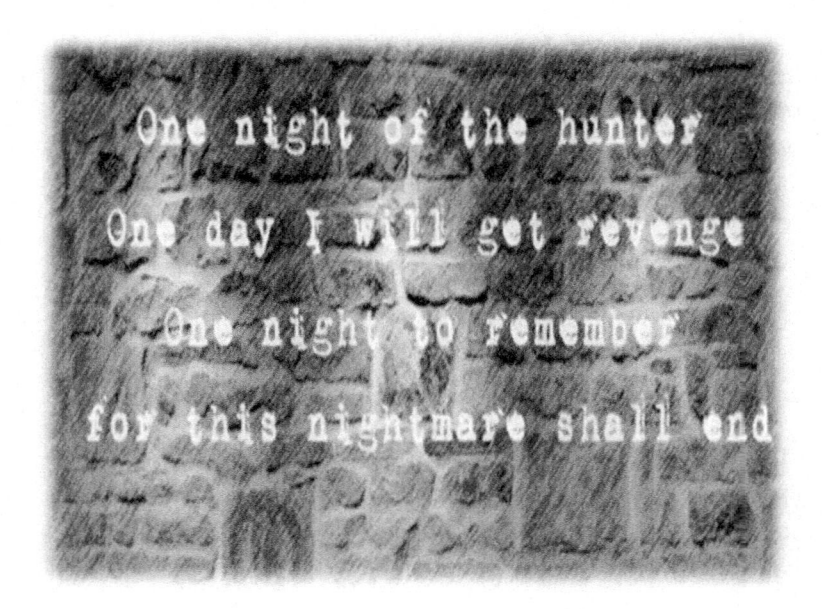

> One night of the hunter
> One day I will get revenge
> One night to remember
> for this nightmare shall end

chased before, only this time the purpose was different. The air was chilling to my bones and the outfit I wore kept me as warm as possible. Each step towards the opening of the woods conjured memories of those who attempted to kill me. My revenge was closer than ever before, and I was more than prepared. The closer I was to the opening of the forest; I could hear the laughter sifting through the air and coldness of the night.

Dressed like a thief in the evening, the path across the field felt as if forever was left behind. The moment was in front of me and as I slowly walked into the opening, I could see an accumulation of twenty teens. Several of them surrounding a small fire, while others were scattered close together. Despite the number of years that surpassed since my last visit, everything appeared to look the same. I kept quiet in the distance seeking those responsible for my attempted murder. From what I could find, three of the five boys were present. Coincidentally, Todd, Jason and Wayne would be standing near one another. They were laughing, drinking and smoking and conversing with others nearby. Kneeling on one knee, I harnessed the memory which brought me here with angry thoughts, callous fear and a strong purpose. There was no going back, and this declaration of intent was the fury from a judge, jury and executioner.

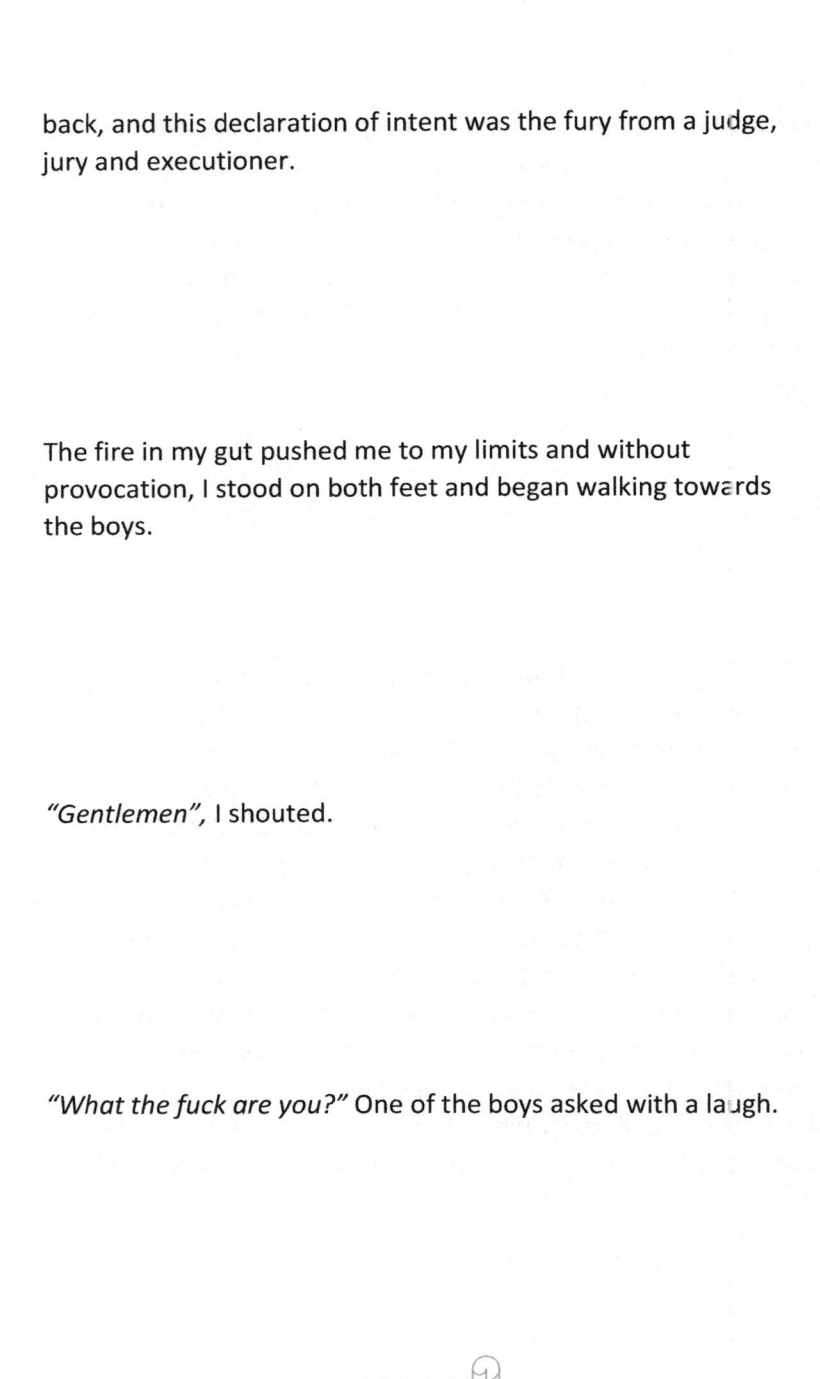

The fire in my gut pushed me to my limits and without provocation, I stood on both feet and began walking towards the boys.

"Gentlemen", I shouted.

"What the fuck are you?" One of the boys asked with a laugh.

"Hey look everyone, it's the asshole in a mask", someone from the crowd stated.

Jason was the tall one of the three and he stood in the middle of his friends. Wearing a New England Patriots jacket, he stood out the worst in my eyes. The other two buffoons wore matching red sweatshirts and had a blank stare in their faces. Most of the teens in attendance were females, so the extra eyes were going to witness my wrath against the cursed boys. Without fear of others being hurt, I concentrated on the three bullies with precise tunnel vision. Standing near the fire, the twenty something teens were faced with a confusing consequence inside of the eyes of a ski mask. Just like something out of a horror movie, the fear among them began to subside and action needed to be taken.

Jason took the immediate brunt of my anger as I walked up and injected a front kick to his stomach. The sound of the force could be heard from miles away as his body was pushed several feet backwards and dropped to his knees. Collecting his breath and wincing in pain, his friend Todd stood to his left. Astonished by his friend on the ground, the small teen moved out of the way and stumbled upon the dirt. His fear was electric, and it stood out in the freezing air because it was welcomed with open arms. He was my next focus as I reached down and grabbed him by his hair and stood him to his feet. With quick precision, I struck him with my right fist against his left eye. Without the chance to cover his face, my left fist penetrated his blocking arm and struck him against the right side of his cheek. Stepping back, I launched a roundhouse kick, connecting with one side of his skull. The brunt force of my kick knocked the young teen to the ground in an instant. The thud-like perseverance pounded the ground like a rock and Todd remained down during the brief altercation.

Looking down upon my victim, I felt nothing towards the boy, despite his cries to stop. Without notice, I felt a sharp pain against the back of my head. Turning around, Wayne had hit me with a large branch that broke into several pieces. The pain subsided quickly, and I launched a full-frontal attack with both hands and legs. Wayne suffered the worst beating of the three as the relentless punches and kicks lasted mere seconds. The chill in the winter night provoked the armory of skills and punches as my breathing failed to waver. I was in the best shape of my life, and I took my anger out on the one person who failed to defend himself.

Both arms and hands remained quick to strike as Wayne fell to the ground, bleeding from his nose, mouth and the few opened wounds from his face. Just as I had suspected, Jason had a piece of wood in his hands, and he was uncoordinated like a small girl. I wasn't sure if I should laugh at him or hold his hand, but my anger took precedence.

"What the fuck do you want?" Jason asked with tears falling from his face.

"I want your life", I replied.

"What did we ever do to you?" He asked.

I understood my compromise, while they clearly misunderstood my silence. I wanted to hurt this piece of shit with all my heart, and nothing was going to stop me. Taking a defensive position, I gestured toward the coward to make a move. On cue, Jason swung the piece of wood and missed as badly as anyone could. I couldn't believe this loser was part of my assault and just as he remained opened after his swing, I kicked his right side with my left leg. The force of the kick moved Jason further away and he swung the branch once again. Unaware of his balance, the swing launched him straight to the ground below. He was out of breath and clearly in disarray. I sort of felt bad for him, but my focus was on the boy who nearly killed me. This sack of shit at the rouse of my angst was close to taking my life and I had to make this fucker pay. His spikey stupid hair, his boyish grin and the sleek appearance applauded for attention, and I was obliging.

Just as I was trained, I stood silent and waited for this coward to make his move. The onlookers were praising him to stand up for himself and he connected with a right punch to my awaiting cranium. Positioning my head downwards to connect with his fist, the sound of broken bones shattered his hand. The jolt shook my spine, but the feeling was intense. Jason wasn't aware of his injury, but I heard it clear as day and so did everyone else. The sound of a broken bone was horrifying and the connection from his punch created several small fractures. The cold air was unfair to determine the extent of any wound, but the numbing helped Jason forget the pain for a moment. Attempting to reconnect, I blocked his next few punches with ease. The last punch would evade its intended target and open my opponent to a throat chop. The brunt of my power against his esophagus cut the air supply to his lungs. Grabbing his throat, Jason bent down and I grabbed him in a headlock and fell backwards towards the ground. The wrestling move was cheesy, but extremely effective. I was pretending to be Jake the Snake Roberts while pushing all my weight on top of his head as it hit the ground. Since I was overly aggressive, I literally thought I almost ripped his head off. Landing on top of him, I rolled over to view the damage. The bully was laying there snoring as I had knocked him out and my attention shifted elsewhere.

Wayne had found himself stumbling to his feet and unaware of his whereabouts. A concussion had slowed his movements and I was sure he needed more of a beating. Slowly walking towards me, I slowly jumped in the air and jolted a downward kick on his left knee. The popping sound was as deafening as his screams while he grabbed for his injured leg.

I reached behind my shirt and grabbed both sticks and began using them on the boy below me. Each stick attacked my opponent fiercely and willingly, like a ninja with mental focus. The kata I had trained for controlled my breathing and the limp body of my enemy received a welcoming attack. The sounds of a thick piece of wood being pounded against flesh is terrifying and the pain was mesmerizing to witness while everyone who remained, saw my wrath. If I was lucky, maybe a few of them would remember what they witnessed when I was the victim before. Each strike against the remaining bully fueled the resilience inside of me. The attack was brief and just as I had finished, I held the sticks in one hand and walked into the night. The steps away from their demise was inviting, and I had conquered something I desperately needed.

Not one person knew the assailant who struck his will upon their three friends, and it would remain that way for many years to pass. Vengeance had a name and to this very day, the other two involved in my beating never answered for their crime. It is not like I didn't attempt to gather the information needed to locate these bullies. I would spend over twenty years trying to locate them, but to no avail.

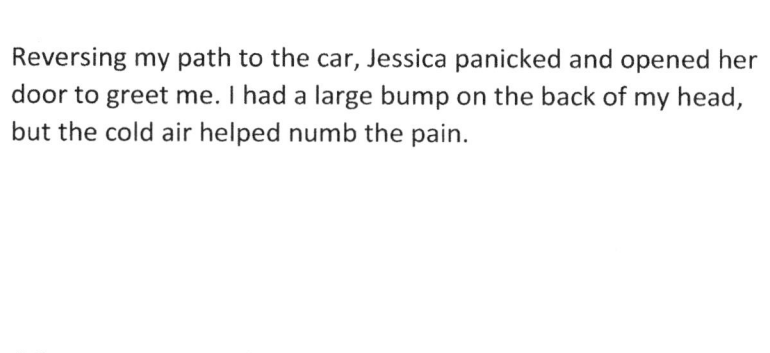

Reversing my path to the car, Jessica panicked and opened her door to greet me. I had a large bump on the back of my head, but the cold air helped numb the pain.

"Shawn, are you ok? I was worried about you", she mentioned with chattering teeth.

"Let's get out of here before we receive more company", I mentioned.

The drive home hid the large smile on my face and with Jessica beside me temporarily, it was time to act on phase two. I had conjured the entire plan for tonight and with tomorrow upon us, I had a lot more in store for the bullies at Masconomet.

Sunday morning arrived and my parents had left town with my sister. It was a rare occasion that I was left at home alone. My mother was scared shitless ever since the incident in 1985, crippling her security of life. We had lived in the small town of Lamarque, Texas because Gary was stationed in Galveston Being a military brat had its advantages and disadvantages. It was a typical beautiful winter day, and my parents were out Christmas shopping. My sister and I decided to clean the house as a present for the assholes who raised us.

I want you to understand one thing as you read this story. was only twelve years old, and my sister just turned ten. We had no business being alone, let alone cleaning the house. Gary and his wife rented the three-bedroom home for us and since he was a terror in our house, we had to keep things clean. On this day for some reason, we felt it necessary as dumb ass kids to clean our parents' bedroom.

While we spent the morning tidying things up, my sister found a Lysol can we used to spray through the air. This is the eighties people, so get used to the Lysol, because that is all they had. Anyway, I noticed a lighter on my mother's dresser and as I grabbed it, the family cat jumped on their bed. When we went to retrieve the feline, the scared critter hid underneath the bed. Equipped with a lighter and a Lysol can, my sister and I attempted to scare the cat under the bed. Before you go crazy on us as kids, let's just say it wasn't a good idea. The flame quickly attached itself to the bottom of the insulation of the bed. Before we could blink, the entire piece of furniture blew up in flames. The beauty of the fire was something out of a movie and my sister and I began noticing the cloud of smoke engulfing the room. We immediately escaped to the confines of the front yard quickly through the front door. Looking back from the street, the black smoke began protruding from the top of the house and several feet high. Without thinking, I sent my sister back into the house with a rag to recover the cat. I had no idea what made me do it, but I was an animal lover and maybe I didn't care to sacrifice Mandy. I was just thinking my parents were going to be pissed because we killed the cat.

The result was a charred home and we nearly lost everything we had. My mother was a wreck and Gary was attempting to salvage anything he could. If you look on the bright side, I was able to save my Atari gaming system and a set of encyclopedias. Not all was lost on my end, and we would eventually move to another town and inherited a babysitter for many years to come. Why today was different, I couldn't tell, but my parents had noticed a huge change in my attitude. My grades were vastly improved and since I arrived home late, they evaded my presence and left early. It could have been the six o'clock visit in the morning from my mother, who saw Jessica lying beside me. Whatever the reason, it gave me time to sit down with Jess at the dinner table and go over my next move. Despite the success of the night before, the next phase was on me, and I had to act quickly.

Chapter 11
A Beautiful Lie

The morning had surpassed the incident of the previous night and I didn't give one shit about it. I was motivated to come into school on Monday and meet with the principal. I had pre-planned this entire weekend as a cover and everything was working as scheduled. Jessica was the key to everything, and she was about to catch a small sample of my hatred for a few students at our High School.

"What happened last night?" She asked while pouring a cup of coffee.

"How long have you known me, Jess?" I asked.

"Long enough, I think. I know a little and was hoping I could learn more", she smartly replied.

"Since I moved here a few years ago, not one person has taken the time to ask why I moved here, and it is frustrating", I mentioned.

"Ok. Good point mister. Why did you move here?" She sarcastically asked.

"Last night, you and I arrived at the Junior High School I had previously attended. For some strange reason, a classmate by the name of Linda decided to share some information with her boyfriend about me. Unaware of her relationship, I took it upon myself to call her one evening and share my feelings. Instead of a welcome the following morning, I was greeted with hatred and a nasty rumor. This red-headed piece of shit decided to inform her boyfriend of my escapade and made it worse than it should have been", I implied.

"Let me guess. Her boyfriend and his friends beat you up in school?" She rudely interrupted.

"Something like that. But any who, I was placed into an awkward situation because this idiot's mouth was too big. Think about it for a minute. Remember the situation in the movie, Karate Kid? All Daniel did was talk to Ally and the ex-boyfriend took it all the wrong way. Eventually, Johnny and his friends would torment Daniel because he flirted with her. This situation is basically the same and the result was a bit different in real life", I stated with purpose.

"I totally get it now. Well, how do you feel now after last night?" She asked.

"Besides this massive bump on my head, I am good. I don't want to talk about it ever again and I want to focus on something else Jess", I replied.

"You have my full attention. What is on your mind?" Jessica asked.

"Over the last couple of years, I have been entangled with a few bullies that have made my life a living hell", I replied.

"Are you referring to Duane and his friends?" She asked with confidence.

"Maybe. How did you know?" I asked her.

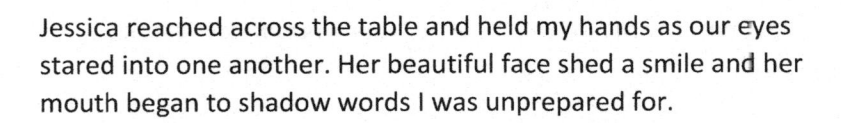

Jessica reached across the table and held my hands as our eyes stared into one another. Her beautiful face shed a smile and her mouth began to shadow words I was unprepared for.

"I only know because Christina feeds me a lot of information about Duane and their relationship. As a matter of fact, you must have done something recently because he is wicked pissed at you", Jessica offered.

"Let's just say I gave him a dose of his own medicine", I repl ed.

"I am sorry you have been dealing with these jerks. I wish I had been with you all those years ago, because they would have left you alone", Jessica stated.

Looking into her eyes, I knew she was telling the truth and now I was at an impasse. The intention for her to remain in my life was for revenge, but it appeared she was on my side. Without hesitation, I continued the conversation with little to offer because I still didn't trust her.

"I want you to just sit back and listen tomorrow during school when they make announcements, ok?" I offered.

She nodded her head in agreeance and I began to catch a feel for everything she knew about Duane and his friends. We would spend the next couple of hours exchanging useful information about my bullies and their life. It was hard to believe this all started with a stupid confrontation in the lunchroom my freshman year. It was no secret Duane was a bully to others in school and he was finally meeting his match. According to Jessica, Duane and his minions were looking for an opening to get their revenge. With that in mind, I offered up my regimen and running schedule to Jessica. It was her idea to bring it to her friend so Duane could offer whatever he thought he could bring. Starting in the spring, I would begin my strict running schedule from the Nike Site to the small downtown area of Topsfield. The captain had me in shape and for me to continue training on my own, running was the root of all success. Jessica wanted to offer my regimen in exchange for keeping her friendship with the small circle of friends. Jessica and I agreed to keep our relationship secretive to prevent her from losing those same friends she had kept close for years.

The pact with my girlfriend was set and when Monday came around, my appearance at the principal's office was the start of our new plan. The previous night I borrowed my mother's typewriter and conjured a special message to be read aloud to the student body. I had already spoken to principal Smith about the weekend, and he was expecting my visit. I found myself in his office the previous week prepping him for a fictitious karate tournament I was invited to. I told him the NKA (National Karate Association) was the host and I had made up the acronym to pass the story as truthful. I had no idea if there was really a tournament, but since I had a good reputation through school, principal Smith had no reason to think otherwise. He appeared excited for me and asked to bring the results to him if I had success at the tournament. The plan was set in motion to take place on the same weekend I hunted my bullies in Weymouth.

This was a perfect cover and upon entering his office, the smile on my face dictated the moment.

Handing him the letter I had typed the night before; principal Smith read the results and became infatuated with spreading the word. I want to be very clear in stating I had no idea this fucking dumb ass was going to tell everyone in school. I anticipated he would, so that is why I shared the information with Jessica. In a perfect world, principal Smith would offer the information to Masco in exchange for buying more time. Did I just say that? I sure did because I needed time to set my plan in motion. Once the letter was handed over, Mister Smith was on his own volition and if he decided to offer the news, it was on him. I sat in the homeroom class and without hesitation, Mister Smith offered the story word for word.

"Good morning, Masco. I want to take this time to congratulate one of our students for competing and winning the National Karate Tournament in New York over the weekend. He is now the recipient of a $50,000 college scholarship and will be

attending BC in 1991. Please take time today to congratulate junior Shawn Wallis on a huge victory as he is now ranked number one in the United States junior division", principal Smith announced.

I could easily have repeated each word spoken from the loudspeaker, but I remained silent. The reaction of my classmates in homeroom was epic and the words had reached the entire student body of the school. During the entire day, I was reminded by my classmates with congratulations and massive attention. It was an anxiety I could live with, but the purpose of the announcement was fulfilling its reason. As we previously agreed, Jessica and I met after school at the library in town. My friend Ken dropped me off and I entered the front door of the library, and her beautiful face greeted me with a smile.

"Holy shit Shawn. That was quite an announcement", she whispered.

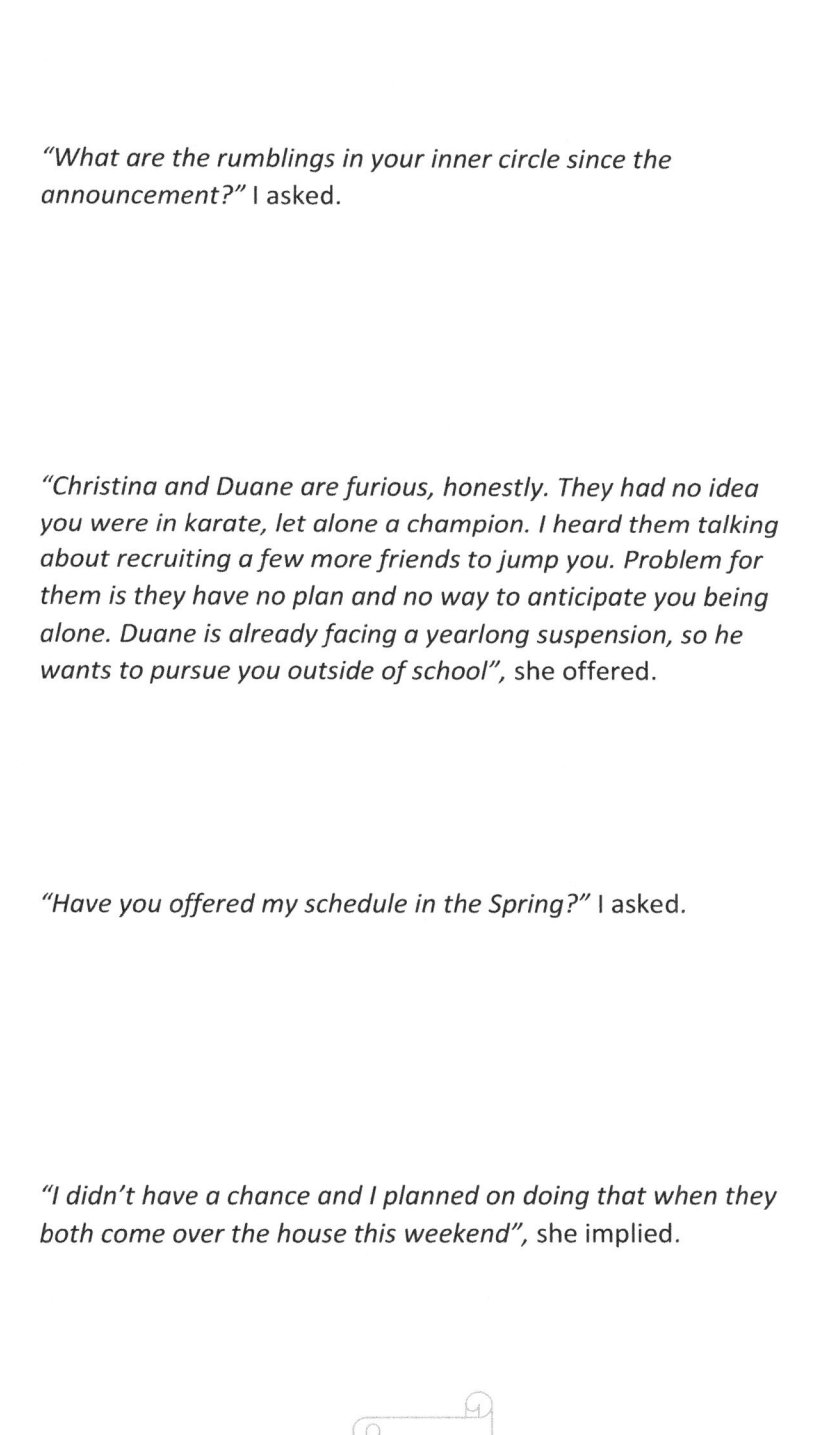

"What are the rumblings in your inner circle since the announcement?" I asked.

"Christina and Duane are furious, honestly. They had no idea you were in karate, let alone a champion. I heard them talking about recruiting a few more friends to jump you. Problem for them is they have no plan and no way to anticipate you being alone. Duane is already facing a yearlong suspension, so he wants to pursue you outside of school", she offered.

"Have you offered my schedule in the Spring?" I asked.

"I didn't have a chance and I planned on doing that when they both come over the house this weekend", she implied.

"Jessica. If they find out we are together, they may kill you. We must be more careful here", I mentioned.

"Why do I feel as if I am being used here Shawn?" She cried.

"Jessica, seriously? If I was using you, I wouldn't offer to protect you or try to put myself in danger by telling you all this information. I am concerned we may make a mistake and they will find out", I explained.

"Shawn. Look at me and I am going to say this only once. I care about you and always have. It isn't my fault you took forever to be in my life. A part of me thinks you approached me to get close to Duane and I don't care. It was a good reason, and I am *accepting of that. It is on you to keep me and not push me away. You have me and I want you to promise me something. Once your plan is set in place and all of this is done, we come out of hiding. Can you please agree to that?"* She asked with purpose.

Holding her hand, I looked down at her beautiful fingers and brought my sites into her eyes and nodded in agreement.

Jessica was on her way home and my confidence in her part of the plan was high. The beautiful lie was the second phase of my plan and before the last part would take place, I had a track season to complete.

The winter was brutal, and we had missed a total of a week or more from school. I took the time to run through the Nike site each day with the confidence of a prince. When school was in session, the announcement created a more popular setting for me to roam through the halls. What I wasn't anticipating was the negative attention it could bring later, but I could care less. I was flying high in the hallways and Jessica, and I were seeing each other as often as we could. I never once imagined finding anyone worth spending time with since I attempted a relationship with a girl name Alyssa Horsfield the previous year. She was a red-headed classmate of mine and I still have no idea what attracted me to her. She had no personality; her parents were weird, and her sister was more attractive. The brief escapade lasted a couple of months, but sports and school took precedence, so I ended the relationship. Today was different because what intended on being a short encounter would blossom into a secret escapade. We liked the same music in hair bands, and we got along easily with great conversations. Jessica was a good girl and she just appeared different than the preppy girls at school. That was something I couldn't understand in school because the cliques were all annoying. Can you imagine attending a school segregated by the way students dressed? It was a matter of stupidity and I pretended to be something I wasn't to fit in. I was dressing in polo shirts to become part of a circle instead of creating my own for others to enjoy. This was the hugest regret I had in high school, and I was a rebel to most people. Here I was a fake karate champion with a huge target on my back and who wouldn't want to be a part of that?

Jessica made me feel wanted for the first time and it was a shame I couldn't share those feelings with the entire school. A large part of my heart felt victim to the society of our high school and it's numbing cruelty. I knew for a fact that I was the victim of bullying from a few students, but also the faculty. I was not hiding my shame and what could have been a comfortable few years at Masco, turned massively dramatic because of me.

Unphased by the cruel surroundings, I was more popular for the wrong reasons. I knew I didn't belong in most groups at school, so I chose to hide away at times from people. During my three years at Masco, I never attended a dance or activity affiliated with class. I was both an introvert and extrovert and sports became the reason for my appearance with other students. I always blamed Gary Wallis for failing to confront others for their shortcomings. Instead of facing my bullies, I would take the time to hide away. The captain was the reason for my current confidence, and I was prepared to carry that into school my junior year. The year was 1989 and I had succumbed to the cruelty of some of the teachers and students because of the abuse I had suffered at home. When my junior year began, I extracted all the fear from my life and walked tall inside of the hallways. I was fearing nothing, and Jessica helped expose my heart, when it failed to recognize her in the past.

Secretly, her friends began noticing her attention towards me and they were happy. It was the miserable string of relationships in her life that chased her into believing boys were the devil. Her parents reminded her of themselves and their success, so Jessica remained keen to the idea. In some way, Duane and his fixation of me helped us find each other and it would be a memory worth building.

The plan to invite Masco into my fake life was about to take a huge turn in the wrong direction. The attention of two classmates would bring to light the truth of my escapade and the walls around me began closing. Their names were Doug Prouty and Daryl Hemeon and they were fucking clueless. They were considered the part of the snobby clique of our class, and I disliked them instantly. In the few years at Masco, I said no word to either, but they frightfully invited themselves into a conversation with my ego, and the shit hit the fan.

"Shawn, can we have an interview with you for the school newspaper?" Doug asked.

"Are you telling me in the three years I have been here, you fuckers have a newspaper?" I rudely asked.

You could tell Doug and Daryl were nervous because they were probably thinking I could snap their necks like a twig. Daryl was a small-framed punk with nice hair and part of Masco's successful soccer team. As a member of the football team, we all disliked soccer and their bullshit tradition of thinking they were better than everyone. If I had it my way, I would beat the shit out of each player and remind them of their place in our school. The memory was nice to have and as Doug was attempting to interview me, I stopped him immediately.

"Your name is Dave, right?" I sarcastically asked.

"It's Doug", he softly responded with a whisper.

"Aren't you a member of the soccer team here?" I asked.

"Yes, I am", me quickly mentioned.

"I will say this Dan. How about you get out of my face and go back to where you came from. How does that sound?" I fiercely stated.

"For the last time, my name is Doug. And whatever. Principal Smith is the one that asked me to interview you", he responded

I reached out and grabbed him by his shirt and pulled him closer with both hands while Daryl looked on.

"Let's be clear. I don't like you and you don't like me. So, stop pretending you want to be here and go back to your asshole of a principal and shove this interview up both your asses", I shouted.

It was obvious I didn't like him and as I let him go, he adjusted his Harvard grey sweatshirt and walked away with his buddy Daryl. Just when I thought that was over, I was called into the office of the principal over the intercom minutes later. What the fuck did this prick want now?

I slowly walked the length of the entire high school and strolled into his office as if I didn't have a care in the world.

"Mister Wallis, please have a seat in my office", principal Smith offered.

I followed him to the opening of his office and both Daryl and Doug were in attendance. Sitting calmly, I walked near Doug's direction and offered the stare from hell. The small flinch I offered shook his confidence and I wanted to terribly to beat his face in and he knew it.

Sitting beside the two students, principal Smith took his seat behind his large desk and offered his words of praise to us all.

"Shawn, I got to hand it to you son. You are good. I called the NKA, and they said they never heard of you. Can you kindly explain?" He asked.

"Nope", I responded sarcastically.

"What is with this kid's attitude?" Darryl asked.

"Hey Hemeon. Why don't you let the adults talk asshole", I aggressively replied.

I looked over at both the idiots in the back of the room and I wanted to stand up and make them piss their pants.

"I want to say that I am very disappointed in your explanation Shawn. You are dismissed", he directed.

I lifted myself from the confines of the comfortable leather seat and turned back towards the two students. I looked at Daryl and Doug with a look of disappointment and turned away and never saw them again. They were attempting to investigate something they had no business looking into and I was offering nothing. Their small newspaper would never be given the chance to print a retraction and the story would remain alive. If I was going to make an example of these students investigating me, I would ruin my reputation. I couldn't take the chance; thus, I began to focus on the indoor track team. Despite the principal's disgust for me, he had no choice but to relinquish his feelings and move forward with the school year.

Chapter 12
The Perfect Weapon

I was considered the co-leader of the hurdles on the indoor track team with Brian Lindquist, and we were fully loaded. Lance Russel, Dave Winship, Dan Alperin, and many others were set to lead one of the most successful track teams in Masco history. The underclassmen made up most of the track team and we appeared ready for anything. During the winter months, each opponent regretted facing our team in the events of the 50-yard dash, 50-yard hurdles, shot put, high jump and the long-distance competitions. We were a unit to be reckoned with and secretly, I was competing in three separate events. The prior year, I was quick over the hurdles, but this year something changed drastically. The captain had offered me a strength that I utilized in my legs, and I noticed quickly. We spent the first few weeks practicing in both the gym and the hallways. Without hesitation, I noticed I had become faster and coach Carletti took notice. I was more agile, crisp, and fluent in my motion over the hurdles. I glided like an eagle over the competition in practice and was escalated into other events on the team. When it came to volunteers for the high jump, I figured I could help. I had no idea what it took to be successful in the high jump, but I found out the hard way. Literally during practice, I swear I hit the fucking high bar twenty times out of twenty jumps. Coach Carletti exuberated patience and took the time after practice to instill a better form in my jump. Once the first week passed, I was beginning to master the event and our team walked into the first competition with high spirits.

Coincidentally, we would score 52 points each week for the first month of the season. It was the fourth meet that brought our team two school records and a phenomenal win against archrival North Andover. In the beginning of the season, coach Carletti informed us that North Andover was considered the favorites heading into the season. We all marked this date on our calendars and with fortitude and attitude, we fought hard against our opponents. We expected a close match, but we didn't anticipate a shattering record for Danny Alperin in the mile. He ran a finishing time of 4 minutes and 40 seconds and clearly destroyed Masco's previous mark in the mile. Just as the celebration continued against North Andover, I was lined up for the 50-yard hurdles and a destiny deserved. The seven other runners had lined up on each side of me as I graced the center lane. This was my night and I had previously sniffed the school record, but not quite enough. Deep in the pit of my stomach, I was deserving of this moment and as my fingers graced the starting line, my body's mechanics plunged forward.

The sound of the gun launched my body from its squatting position and into the lead with the first hurdle in site. The tunnel of hurdles was closer in my mind, and I ran as if the wind was behind me. Each second on the watch slowly conspiring to prevent history, I was superior on this evening. The five hurdles were no match for my speed and within mere seconds, I surpassed the finish line, placing first. I attempted to celebrate with the other racers until coach approached my direction. He informed me I had shattered the school record by a whole three tenths of a second. The 6.69 seconds were mine to keep, and the personal celebration was short-lived as our team would narrowly escape the town of Lynn against North Andover. The 52-44 final score would propel our team towards the goal of an undefeated season. We were 4-0 and Danny and I were new school record holders and the talk of the school. I had smashed a long-standing record and despite my will to become an All-American on our baseball team, this would suffice. Just when the celebration united our team, coach had some awful news that would literally ruin our season.

According to coach Carletti and his conversation with me upon arriving back at school, my record would not be present on the wall. I was confused, hurt and biased towards the old man who was holding me back. I wanted to choke someone, but who?

"Coach, why are you not posting my record on the gym wall?" I asked.

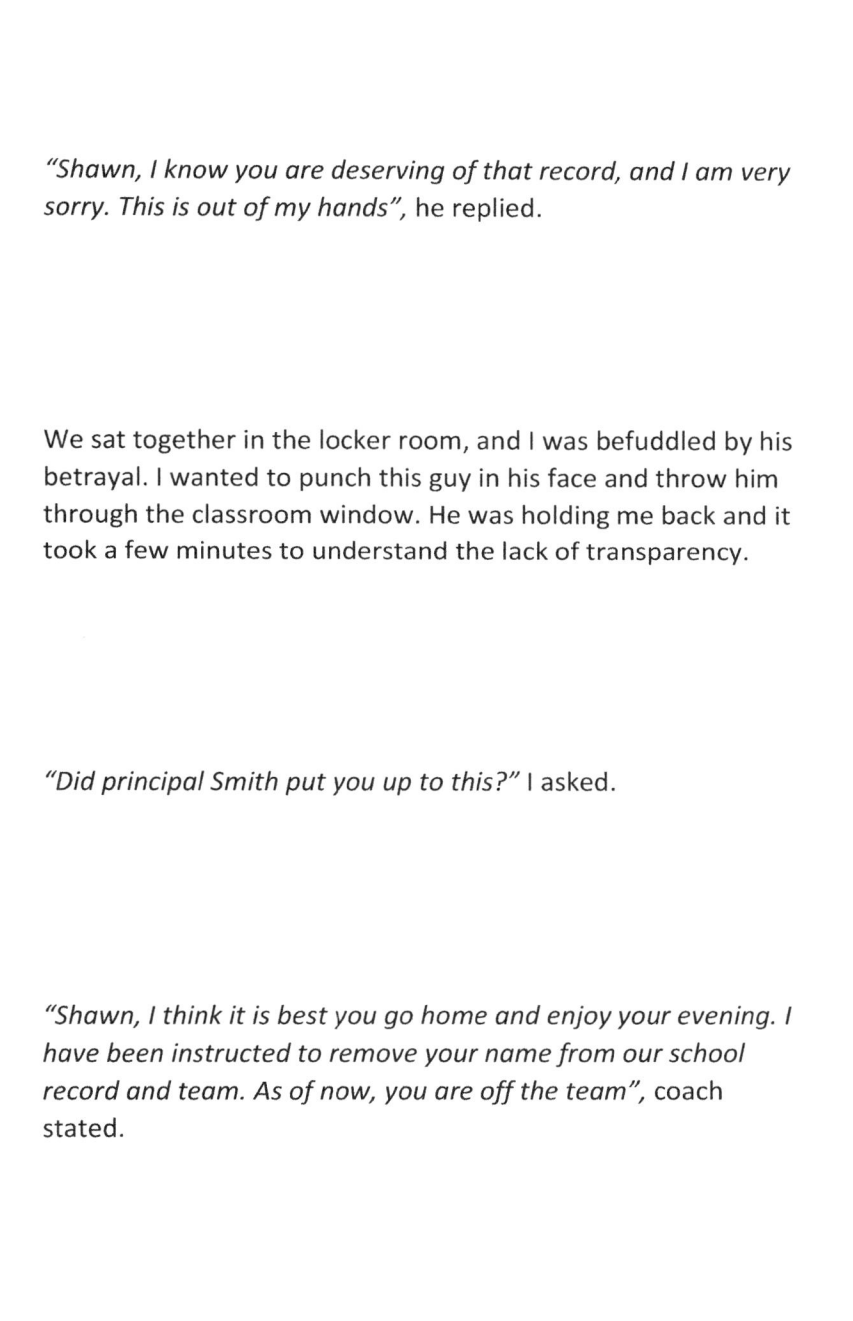

"Shawn, I know you are deserving of that record, and I am very sorry. This is out of my hands", he replied.

We sat together in the locker room, and I was befuddled by his betrayal. I wanted to punch this guy in his face and throw him through the classroom window. He was holding me back and it took a few minutes to understand the lack of transparency.

"Did principal Smith put you up to this?" I asked.

"Shawn, I think it is best you go home and enjoy your evening. I have been instructed to remove your name from our school record and team. As of now, you are off the team", coach stated.

Principal Smith was going to step on my record and there was nothing I could do about it. His embarrassing investigation made a fool of his administration and now I was being punished. How in the world could I become a victim of bullying from one school of students to another and now the faculty was taking their swings. I couldn't win for losing and I took this fight home with me.

I walked into the house after I was dropped off by a fellow teammate. It was unusual for Gary to be home early from his tour, so he greeted me at the door.

"Son, can we talk for a few minutes. There is something on my mind and I need to get it off my chest", Gary mentioned.

I removed my backpack from my shoulder and set it near the front door. Just as I placed it to the ground, Gary decided to put his hands on me and pushed me to the ground.

"What the fuck did I tell you mother fucker. You are not to embarrass me, and this family and you just had to lie to the principal. What in the hell were you thinking Shawn?" He violently asked as he stood above me.

This is what I trained for and as I lay on the ground, I usually just covered my face and waited for Gary to stop hitting me. This was different times and I immediately got to my feet and stood right in front of his face.

"Are you a tough guy now? Do you want me to kick the shit out of you again?" He shouted.

Without provocation, Gary raised his right hand and attempted to hit the side of my face with his fist. Easily blocking his strike to the right of my body, I reached for his arm and wrist, and performed a lock. This was to use his own power against him, and it worked to perfection. Pinning the abusive asshole to the wall, I raised my left leg and slammed it hard on the back of his right knee. The pressure of my power buckled his leg and he fell to the ground below me. Stepping back, Gary suddenly saw red and got back to his feet in a hurry.

The forty-year-old abusive asshole was angry, and he lunged at me from the front door area. Grasping my shirt, it ripped completely, and my bare chest was exposed to his sharp nails. The pain subsided quickly while a few streams of blood soaked my stomach. I looked down and before I could look up, Gary was assaulting me with several punches. The first two landed on my chest, but I recovered quickly and began defending his attacks. One by one, his punches were rendered meaningless as they struck the air in front of me and to my side. Gary was no longer in control and with a quick front kick, I pushed him to the brink. Just as he attempted to catch his breath, I arrived with a flurry of front punches and unique speed. In total, I would land fifteen hits and Gary fell straight to the ground and lay defeated. I could have easily continued and beat him to a pulp, but I did the smart thing and dialed 9-1-1. I wanted this man to suffer and when the cops arrived, so did Jessica.

The cops interviewed me as I was being tended by the EMT's. My chest was bruised and battered, and my soul was feeling invincible. Gary was no longer the aggressor after tonight and if he ever put his hand on me again, I would literally blind him. That was the message I had for him as I stood in the street and waited for Jessica to gather a few of my clothes. The darkness was upon the Nike Site and instead of going to Jess's home, I asked her to bring me to Jeff Milk's house. I thought it was too early to involve Jess in my drama and because she was amazingly helpful, I would invite myself over a lot.

The knock on the door was enticing and Jeff's mother answered. I needed help and the stitches and bandages provided the silent excuse for shelter. The family always liked me and after explaining my situation, they offered their home for as long as I needed. I was sure to mention how abusive Gary was, but I decided to withhold what I had done to him. I had no intentions of scaring anyone in town over my anger. I had become the perfect weapon and I didn't want to place myself in a miserable situation. Jeff was my friend, and it was his family's hospitality that allowed me to heal quickly. I would eventually stay with the family for a period of five weeks during weekdays and at Jessica's for the weekends. I honestly had no clue what I was doing, but I felt miserable because I was invading my friend's personal space. Jeff had a girlfriend named Gretchen Hover and she was an athlete like us at Masco. My intention was to continue coming straight from school to Jeff's house, train until the evening and head to bed. This would continue for weeks, and Jeff began to take notice of my transformation.

"Got a second Shawn?" he asked as I nodded.

"Not like it is any of my business, but did you assault your father?" He asked.

"Don't tell anyone Jeff, but I had no choice. He assaulted me and I defended myself", I replied.

"Defended yourself? You nearly put the man in intensive care. How did you learn how to fight like that?" He asked.

"Yeah. I learned a couple of moves from watching the Karate Kid, no big deal", I sarcastically replied.

"The cop that interviewed your mother is a family friend and she says it a bit differently. Just so that you know what's going around", Jeff replied.

"Jeff, honestly? I was trained to defend myself by a concerned person in my life and I am glad I did. He is a good man and he just suddenly left town", I mentioned.

"Interesting", he replied.

"Don't judge me, Jeff. If it wasn't for my master, I would probably be dead in that home", I replied.

"Are you telling me the tournament you were in was real?" He asked.

"Let's just say something was real, but the event took on another story of its own. I mean no harm Jeff to anyone, and I needed to make changes for the better", I replied.

"Rumor has it you were sexually assaulted by Duane White and a couple of his friends. I only know because Gretchen is friends with a few people that know him. He has been bragging about it for a long while. I am sorry that happened to you", Jeff scarcely implied.

"I rather not talk about that. It was something that happened, and I still have plans on doing something about it", I stated.

"Whatever you plan on doing, I think you already accomplished that when you attacked him recently. Be very careful Shawn. These druggies have ulterior motives that may hurt you or someone you care about, like Jessica. Can you be careful long enough to stay alive?" Jeff mentioned.

Unwilling to capture my hint, Jeff was now a part of phase three. I hadn't intended on using him to help me because I was attempting to get Rick Anthony's help another way. Since Gary decided to show his face, I was now in the driver's seat and the plan was ready for the taking.

"Jeff, how about I confront Duane in the morning on my own with you and the guys behind me. You know, to help prevent outside interference. That way, the school can bear witness to this bully succumbing to his own victim", I mentioned.

"That is a hell of an idea. Why didn't I come up with that? Tell you what. I will get a hold of a few guys and we will all meet at my locker at homeroom. Duane and his druggy friends always hang there", Jeff offered.

"This meeting should be the last of the bullying from Duane and his loser friends. I was clear in the locker room that I was not going to stand for his bullshit. If you can help me by being there, I will handle the rest. No matter what happens Jeff, do not get involved. If anyone else decides to interfere, just be my eyes", I carefully explained.

The deal was in place and Jeff had informed Ken Nazarian, Rick Anthony, Rich Crosson, Lance Russell, Lee Spencer and a few others of my meeting in the morning. It was unexpected for a person needing to be surprised. I was going to confront my school bully once and for all in front of the school and this was my perfect beginning, my inception. I had no intention of being unfair or impartial towards my bully. He was going to finally understand what losing control is all about and without a doubt, I needed this victory. It was phase three and I had one more trick up my sleeve that was wheeling into motion. Jessica and I knew what was in store and she decided to stay home sick. We spoke for a couple of hours that evening and she made me feel alive. She was my unexpected gift, but I had no idea she was about to throw a monkey wrench into the perfect plan.

The morning arrived and came without a hitch. Jeff drove me to school and aware of what was to come, I was ready. The parking lot was a few moments away from the hallway that would be the setting for this once in a lifetime showdown. I just recently took my revenge from the boys in Weymouth, but this was going to be different. I wasn't intending on hiding my face, but rather show myself to the school who was not afraid. The rumors were swirling that Duane had assaulted me and it was time to place those words to bed.

Jeff and I waited at his locker by the stairwell as Ken, Richie and the others began to appear. The hallway appeared smaller by the second and I looked over at the guys with cruel intentions.

My eyes told a story and Jeff knew it was time to face the music. The intervention was about to begin and phase three was upon our lives. I started walking slowly towards the end of the hall, while the guys followed.

"Jeff, what the hell is Shawn doing?" Ken Nazarian asked.

"Patience Ken, patience. Just watch the show, you are in for a treat", Jeff whispered.

"Shawn needs to end this quick. I have a math test", Rich Crosson joked.

Jeff had collected all the muscle in our circle and these guys were there to prevent any issues. From Duane's perspective, a brawl was ensuing, and he was running out of options quickly.

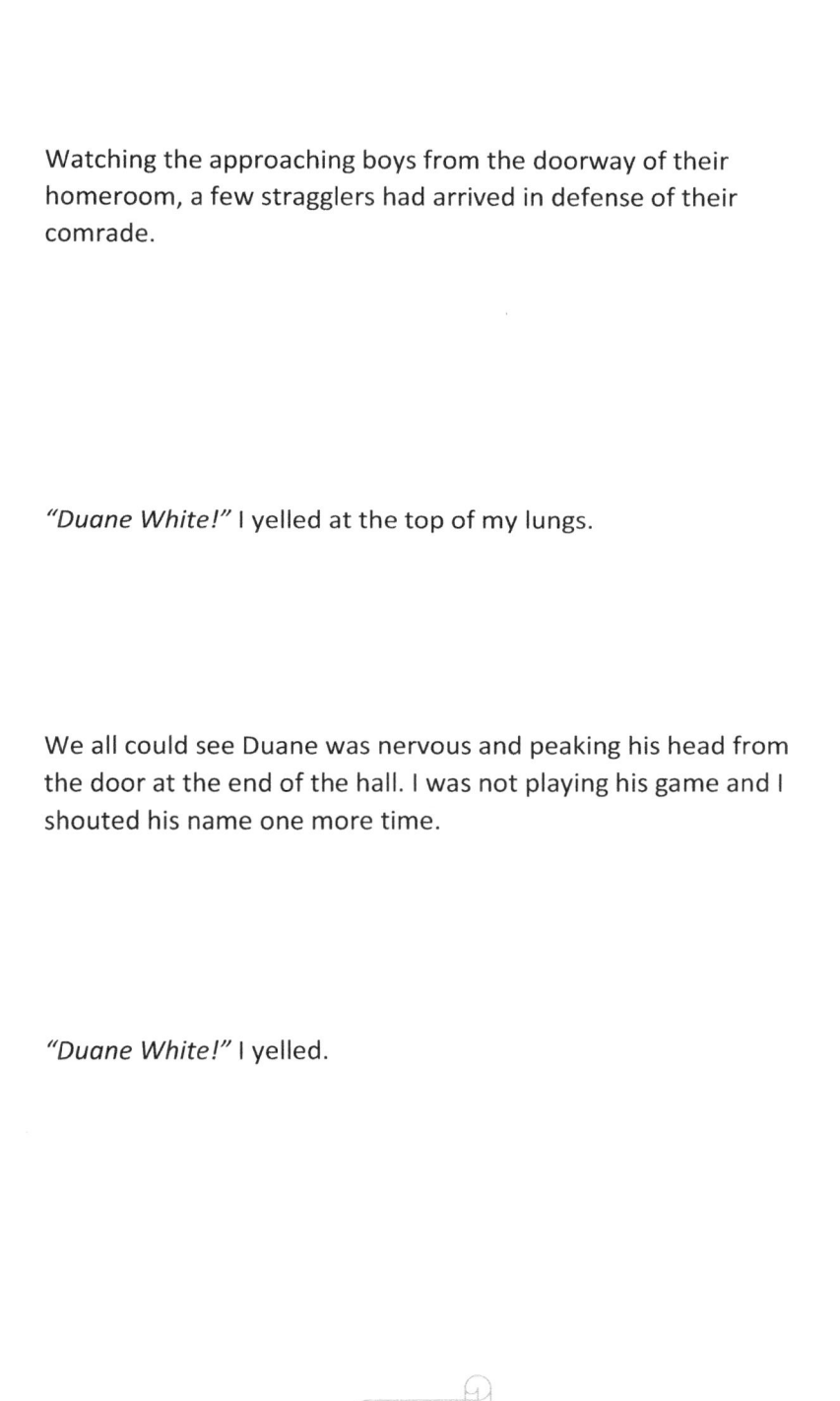

Watching the approaching boys from the doorway of their homeroom, a few stragglers had arrived in defense of their comrade.

"Duane White!" I yelled at the top of my lungs.

We all could see Duane was nervous and peaking his head from the door at the end of the hall. I was not playing his game and I shouted his name one more time.

"Duane White!" I yelled.

Failing to acknowledge my calling, I walked further towards the door. Within a few feet of its opening, Coach Pugh showed his face.

"Shawn, Jeff. What are you all doing here?" Coach asked.

"Nothing much coach. I just wanted Duane to come out and play. Can you stop holding his hand and ask him to come out?" I eerily asked.

Behind coach Pugh, we could all see Duane's silhouette pointing the middle finger and laughing at us. He dodged a huge bullet, and someone tipped him off. I didn't suspect anyone in our own circle of refusing my victory, so my mind wandered.

I knew Jessica was home sick, so I asked Jeff to borrow his vehicle and I immediately drove to see her in Middleton. Gary had spent countless hours teaching me to drive his raggedy car, so I was prepared. Jeff's vehicle was in good hands, but my anger was not. I wanted to know why my new best friend was ruining my glory and it didn't take long to find out.

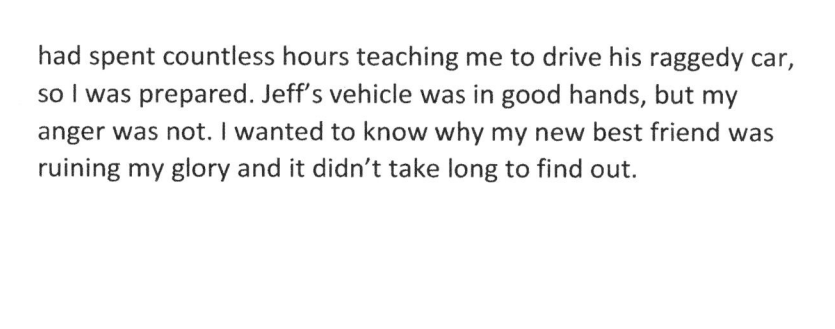

Arriving at her house several minutes later, Jessica greeted me outside.

"Shawn, you can't be here", she stated.

"Why did you sell me out? Why did you tip him off Jessica?" I asked.

"Did you really think I was going to fall for your bullshit and not realize you were using me?" She asked.

"I explained all of that. My first intentions were callous, but then I began falling for you", I offered.

"That is horse shit man. You wanted your revenge and those are my friends. You pissed them off Shawn. Don't you fucking get it. You were the one who initiated the fighting, and you should have just let it be. Now you are going to get your ass kicked and I won't stop them anymore", she rudely stated.

Proving silence was my best option, I turned around with a tear slowly ejecting itself from the corner of my eye and drove away. The vision of Jessica in the rear-view mirror was the last time I would catch a glimpse of the beautiful vixen. Someone in her small circle got a hold of her and turned her against me. This was high school, and it should have been expected. I was prepared for the worst and my plan was to continue with phase four. It was the final phase to supplant my revenge and discontinue the harassment from the bully of Masco.

I arrived back home with the Wallis family and Gary apologized for his demeaning behavior. It was repetitive and unnecessary because I was determined to end his life if he touched me again. For the life of me, I finally was able to stand up to the bully at home and nothing was going to stand in the way of my victory over Duane. For the first time in my life, Gary no longer had control in our household, and I think my sister and mother could breathe easier. What dominated my mind was the constant bullying from the faculty as Masco. Whether it was principal Smith, or coach Kasey, coach Puleo, coach Carletti, or coach Sauchuk. They tormented me as equally as the bullies did over the years and I never forgave them. I entrusted my coaches to strand by their decisions and I was never initially going to capture glory. In baseball, I was considered a prodigy of sorts in the eyes of many in Topsfield, but our coach was blind.

Baseball season was now in full session and as expected, Rick Anthony and I would lead the charge for the 1990 season. He was a senior and somehow, he began taking a step backwards. I couldn't understand his demise, but Rick was not pitching well in practice or his first game. We barely beat Ipswich in the first game, and I knew I had to step up. We won 5-4 and we should have easily won by a lot more runs. Coach Sauchuk was up to his usual bullshit, and I was having none of it. I took it upon myself after Rick's pitching performance to confront Coach in his classroom. Richard Sauchuk was a science teacher, and I never had the luxury to be his student, but since I was not shy of his crappy ability as a coach, it was for the best.

I was angry and I finally ripped into the man that would be responsible for the loss of my future.

"Coach, can we talk for a few minutes?" I asked.

"Why aren't you on the practice field warming up with the others?" He asked.

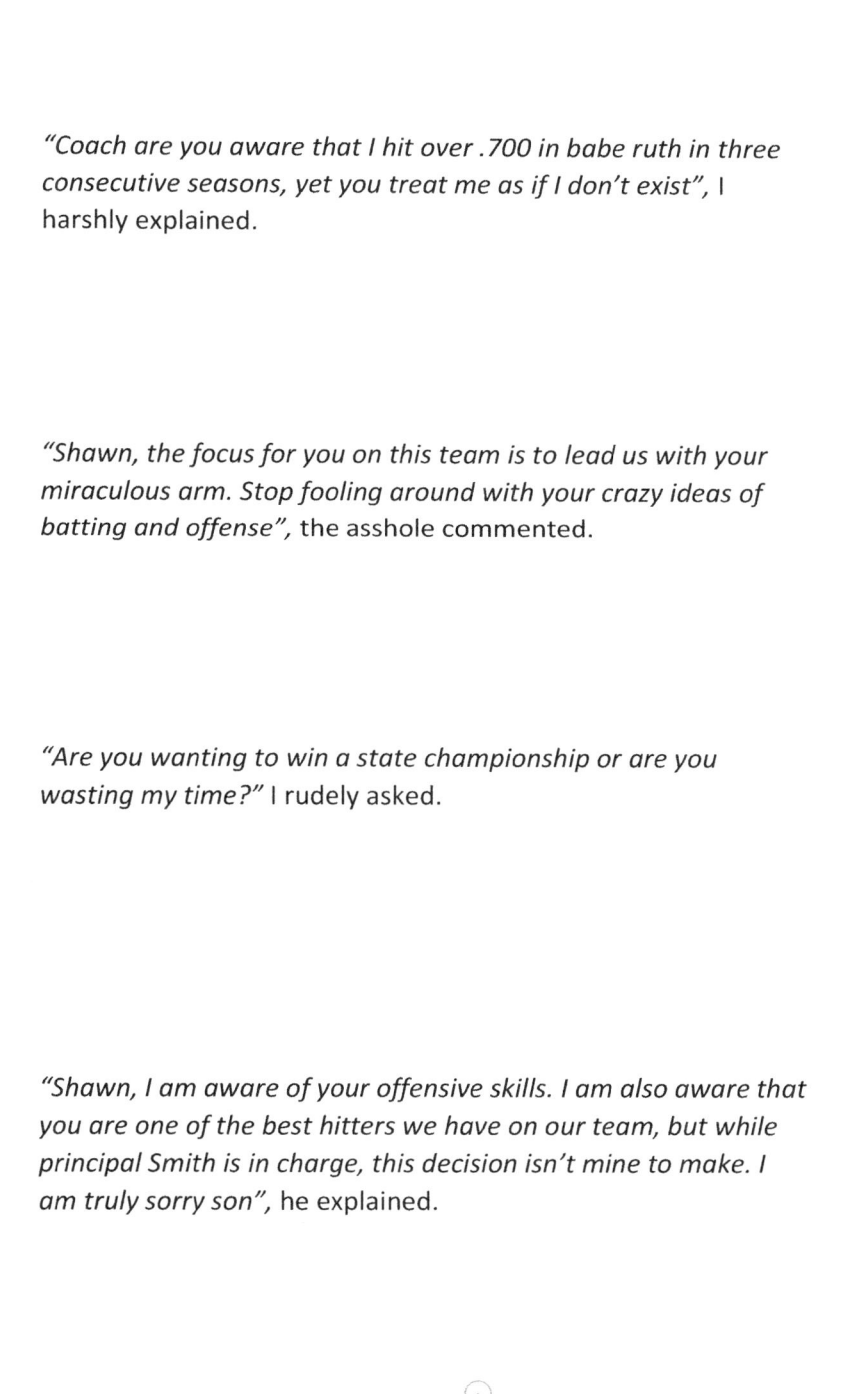

"Coach are you aware that I hit over .700 in babe ruth in three consecutive seasons, yet you treat me as if I don't exist", I harshly explained.

"Shawn, the focus for you on this team is to lead us with your miraculous arm. Stop fooling around with your crazy ideas of batting and offense", the asshole commented.

"Are you wanting to win a state championship or are you wasting my time?" I rudely asked.

"Shawn, I am aware of your offensive skills. I am also aware that you are one of the best hitters we have on our team, but while principal Smith is in charge, this decision isn't mine to make. I am truly sorry son", he explained.

"What the fuck is this guy's deal coach?" I asked.

He didn't have to answer the question because we all knew the answer already. This piece of shit was responsible for blocking my school record and now he was preventing me from helping our team win a championship. Looking at our lineup, we had enough to make it to the State playoffs, but with teams like Drury and Salem waiting, we needed more offense.

"Coach, something is puzzling me. If the principal is behind my handcuff, then why did you keep me off the roster last year?" I asked with purpose.

He was intending on offering the answer and a huge part of me knew who was behind it. For two consecutive years, Masco High School baseball would fall victim to stupidity. We failed to eclipse our potential last year and now we were heading for failure again. There was only one shot here and I took it. I was building up the pressure in my chest to spew the words and without thinking, the sentence was on my lips.

"Coach, this will be my last year here. You will get my best on the mound, but I am announcing my retirement from baseball for good", I stated.

"Shawn, I need you these next two years. You are more than capable of leading us defensively, but I can't in any way put you in the lineup. I could lose my job, benefits, pension, and even my family. I am sorry, but if you choose to walk away, then so be it. I can't stop you. You have an unbelievable talent, and I would hate to see you throw it away, despite my reluctance. I think what is best for you is to remain on the bump and hammer out these wins for us. I know what you are capable of in the batter's box, but this team needs a leader on the mound. If you want to walk away at the end of the season, I can't stop you" Coach murmured as I walked out of the classroom.

Coach thought he was going to run me in the ground the next two years, and he was sadly mistaken. I had enough of the bullshit at this school and it was time to move on. I was attending this school for a few more months and I was on my way. Whether it be at Salem or some other High School, I didn't care. Coach said his peace and I barely listened as I turned around and walked towards the ball field. My anger took over and I would utilize it as my fuel. This school hadn't seen a player like me and with Jeff, Ken and Rick on the offense, I was going to take full advantage of my ability on the mound.

The first game I would pitch was right after Rick's stinker. The team was North Andover, and they weren't prepared for my wrath. I was an angry soul on the bump and when the first pitch cracked Jeff's glove, the invitation of terror was just beginning.

Chapter 13
Pulse of the Maggots

The Cape Ann League was aware of my name from the prior year, but this season was new and so was my ability. My fastball gained quicker speed and the North Andover hitters were having issues all day. I would strike out the side in the first on nine immaculate pitches and the offense prepared to stand behind me, plating three runs and a lead I would never relinquish. Each pitch from my hand would precisely touch the plate and send the batter back to his bench. The scent in the air wreaked of a blooming paradise and I was the lonely man on its island. The fastball and curveball complimented each other like family and not one batter could touch the ball. Except for a dribbler to shortstop, North Andover failed to make contact on nearly every pitch. It was an amazing feat for me on the mound as I surrendered one hit and struck out a career high eighteen batters. We were a team of undefeated teens with one goal in mind and since the school was handcuffing my talent, I chose to propel as a pitcher. My reluctance was inside of my pride, and I swallowed it for the upcoming season. Masconomet had the chance of going undefeated and competing for a State Championship and possibly a national ranking. Our team was considered one of the most talented up until now and our principal was placing a damper on his own students.

While the baseball season was beginning its regular season tilt, I was focused on one person. Duane had eluded me since I confronted him, but there were signs of other's interested in pestering my anxiety. Occasionally, some lame, long-haired, heavy metal t-shirt wearing prick would attempt to bump into me in the hallway. This was a daily event and since you could pick these idiots out like flies, I was more than ready for their assault. Most of the time the occurrences would happen in between classes, and I would easily send them to the ground with a bruised body and damaged ego. When I first attended Masco years earlier, I barely weighed one hundred and forty pounds wet. With time and a few hours in a gym, I would gain over thirty-five pounds and set forth the rock I worked hard to become.

The baseball team finished with twelve wins my sophomore year and without my talent on offense, I projected an improvement of a couple of games this year. Coach wanted to continue using Ken as a pitcher between Rick and I, which made no sense. He was unable to capture glory one time and we easily lost three games with Ken at the helm. Rick was struggling as well with a few losses for the year, so I had no choice but to step my game up for our team and get to the playoffs. The second and third games I pitched in 1990 were shutouts and easy victories. Ipswich and Hamilton-Wenham were reluctant to compete and took a step to the side as we demolished them. Our record was 5-3 when we took on the heavily favored Newburyport team. His name was Jon Story, and he was one of the favorites to win MVP of our league. He didn't have an electric fastball, but he was precise with the one pitch he mastered: the curveball.

This was my personal playoff as I was 3-0 going into the game against John and his team. We hosted the first of two games against this powerful team, and I did not disappoint. As you recall, Newburyport was my only defeat in Cape Ann play my freshman year, so I wanted revenge. They were solid from top to bottom in their lineup and since I had played against them before, I was more prepared. I never pitched against them my sophomore year, so my only defeat was the last time we played against one another.

The game was an immediate chess match during the first two innings. I surrendered no hits while John was matching my every move. When the bottom of the third inning began, Jeff and Rick would smash towering doubles and Ken followed with a walk. This would leave the middle of the order to finally give our team the leverage we needed. Once the game had finished that early evening, we had beaten them 8-2 and I remained undefeated. The game was the talk of the school for days and we had inched closer to a berth in the playoffs. We needed the elusive twelve wins to clinch and with my streak of unbeaten games extended, I figured we would easily walk into the postseason. We were halfway to twelve wins, and I needed Rick to play better and with him winning his next two starts, Masco would find themselves in a game of interesting circumstances at the town of Amesbury.

Gary Wallis noticed the success I was having, and my name was flooding the local newspaper, *The Salem Evening News*. While the wins were piling up, he became more frustrated and annoyed at the attention I was receiving. How dare I supersede the alpha asshole in the house, so he decided to make me pay one day. I was set to pitch against Amesbury High and my knucklehead of a father-wannabe chimed in with his opinion from the stands.

"Come on Shawn! Throw the ball Shawn", he yelled furiously.

"That's not a strike Shawn. Throw a strike Shawn", he shouted at the top of his lungs.

I am literally standing on the mound and his shouting started to bother me. I had dealt with adversity my entire life, but this was beyond immature. Here was this thirty something year old man acting like a two-year-old and I so badly wanted to stop the game and kick him in the face. The man who was supposed to be my guardian, my protector, was now my enemy and I used it to my full advantage. The anger deep within my bones resonated a power I had never felt before and I began raising the speed of my fastball. Jeff Milks noticed behind the plate, and he was perpetually a witness to one of my best career games.

I pitched a fourth shutout of the season and earned the start for the All-Star Game. I was now undefeated with six wins and our team was one game short of the playoffs. Despite all the glory, I stood on top of the mound during each inning of that game and looked over at the man who hated me. I was considered a stepchild to him, but the day he nearly killed me in the front yard never left my dreams. Gary Wallis would begin to haunt my nightmares for years to come and his obedience towards his pedophile father really set me back. My sister was comfortable with the abuse and even thirty years later, I never stopped hating them for it. Seven innings of hell for the man who wanted badly to kill me, and I was happy to oblige.

My teammates could be heard saying awful things about Gary during the game and they didn't faze me one bit. They were all correct and even Rick Anthony was annoyed and said something during the fourth inning. Most of the players from the other team apologized to me at the end of the game and it was much appreciated, despite the shame. I was wicked embarrassed to be associated with his psychopathic ways and I wanted to hurt him terribly.

The drive home was awkward and never did I get a congratulations or anything. This was the same man who spent countless hours catching my fastball in the back yards of our homes over the years. He was always helpful in seeing that I worked hard and mastered my craft. Everything changed in our lives once I became a teenager. Don't get me wrong, he literally almost killed me a few times when I was around the ages of eleven and ten. When I turned thirteen, all bets were off, and Terri and Gary Wallis smashed me with a barrage of physical, mental, and verbal abuses. Things were so bad when I became a teen, that I constantly ran away from home to live in the woods or at a friend's home.

I remember one incident when I was thirteen and living in the small town of Hitchcock, Texas. The town was east of Houston and north of Galveston, while it was a secluded town of oil refineries and good old cowboys. The diversity in our neighborhood was like something I never saw, and I befriended kids with Asian, Afro-American, and Spanish descent. I was happy to be out of the house and enjoying my friendships and comraderies instead of being the focus of daily beatings and verbal attacks.

The night that changed my thinking in life was the time my mother and her drunk husband nearly killed themselves. Apparently, Gary took the keys and attempted to drive home drunk from the Galveston military base bar on a late March evening in 1986. If you recall, my sister and I burned the house down the year prior, so here I am with a fucking babysitter waiting for my drunk parents to arrive home. It was nearly one in the morning when my parents strolled in and appeared in dismay. The story from my mother wasn't clear, but this is what I gathered in all the rampage.

Gary took the keys from my mother and attempted to drive the thirty minutes home. Unclear of the road in front of him, Gary's stupid ass missed the exit for the onramp of the highway and crashed into the side of the pillar of the bridge. My mother did what she could to protect her husband and claimed she was driving. When it came time to withdraw blood at the hospital, she did everything she could to avoid his withdrawal. If Gary had been caught drinking and driving, he would have not only lost his decorated military career, but he would have faced prison in Texas. We lived in a state that did not mess around with drunk drivers and Terri protected the asshole. I wish he had been caught because I wouldn't have suffered the severe abuse I did over the next few years.

Despite the rash of horrible words from Gary during the ball game, the respect for my talent was never questioned and the league had recognized me as one of the best pitchers in the State of Massachusetts. We stood at 13-6 with one more game to be played and all hell was fixing to break loose for the reckless kid with an agenda.

Out of the blue, Jessica called my home and warned me of a potential attack in the morning. She had confessed that she had given Duane and his friends the location of my route and she was sorry. I hung the phone up thinking I would be upset, but I clearly wasn't. After all the careful planning over the years, I was finally desperately needed. Regardless of the amount of friends Duane may bring, this was my chance at redemption. This was my year and mine to hold onto. I trained for this exact moment, despite getting my revenge in South Weymouth. I could care less what was happening south of Boston, but here in Topsfield, a debt was going to be paid.

For me to be prepared for what was coming, I had to be mentally ready. This routine of mine was a regular occurrence for over a period of one year to keep me in game shape for all sports. I would trek my ten-speed bike away from the Nike Site and head north on the one highway that could easily kill me with one mistake. The venture down the hill of route one was something of a roller coaster until I reached the bottom. The strength in my legs were tested once I began heading up the other side of the hill. It was a mountainous road that seemed like an eternity and by the time I came close to the top, I took a left turn on a street called Garden St. The welcoming road was shadowed by enormous trees and beautiful leaves on this crisp morning. The sun was rising perfectly above the horizon and the brisk air was refreshing to my face. My legs and mind were relaxed, and I slowly garnered enough speed to reach the intersection. Taking a right on Hill Street, I would venture for several miles on River and Salem Roads before coming to Prospect Road. This private maze was the easiest way to downtown without playing frogger on the busy highway on route one. My heart was racing in anticipation of the bullies and their mindset. I knew they weren't stupid enough to hide in the bushes along the way, but my assumption would fool me. Just as I began turning onto South Main Street, I placed my bike on the sidewalk on the west side of the road. The house on my left sat on the corner of Prospect Road and South Main St. It was the second house that caught my attention since it appeared someone was hiding behind the tree. Peddling on the sidewalk, I immediately ditched the bike to the left of the driveway of the two-story blue house.

It landed between the first two trees before the driveway, and I slowly walked towards the larger tree in front of the house.

"Come out, come out wherever you are?" I asked out loud.

The tree wasn't wide enough to hide his shadow, but Duane appeared from behind it and stood near the sidewalk.

"How did you know I was here?" He asked while holding a wooden bat.

"Duane, I have always known you were going to be here. The moment you began messing with me, I just knew you would be stupid to come here someday", I exclaimed while slowly walking towards him.

"Why don't you run away like you always do pussy", Duane rudely commented.

"Are you going to ask your friends to come to the party?", I smartly asked.

There was no doubt a fear in Duane's eyes appeared because my confidence was through the ceiling and the bat in his hands kept him safe. Just as I poked the bear, his friend Craig and Jody appeared from behind the house. Walking slowly down the driveway as if they were in the halls of Masco, the two dumb fucks lazily appeared disinterested. Taking advantage of their lack of focus, I immediately went after Craig. He was the weakest of the group, and I wanted Duane all by his lonesome. Standing at the end of the driveway on the sidewalk, I quickly walked onto the grass and performed a roundhouse kick. My body was in perfect position near Craig while my foot landed against his chest, knocking him backwards. The brunt of the force placed Jody in immediate defense. He came at me quickly and his wavy hair and olive skin invited themselves into a mismatched fight. Maybe he thought he was a tough talker, but I had expected a stronger punch into my chest. His right hand came forward and I allowed it to land on my right pectoral muscle. The lack of force caught his hand and allowed me to quickly grab his right wrist and pressure lock it downwards. Snapping like a twig, I nearly shattered his arm into a million pieces as he grabbed himself and fell to the grass. Lifting my leg, I crushed down mightily on Jody's left ankle and crippled him temporarily. The loud crack was spiteful, but very necessary. Craig awaited his turn peacefully and he lunged at me with a weak right cross. When I say weak people, I literally mean it took years to cross in front of my face. This teen was something else and had no business being in Duane's affairs. All I remember was him holding me down while Duane sexually assaulted me, and the anger took over.

I suddenly landed a left to the right side of Craig's face, launching him into the surprised tree in the middle of the yard. Just as I walked towards Craig, I felt a sharp pain against the mid-section of my back. Duane had taken a huge swing behind me and landed perfectly across my lumbar area. The bat was heavy and packed a powerful punch as it took the breath out of me momentarily. Learning what I had been taught, I took a quick breath and punched Craig in the nose as he leaned up against the tree. I had enough time to handle what was in front of me since I no longer wanted anymore surprises.

Turning around, Duane stepped back with the bat in his hands, and I began the approach. While I am walking, I look down at Jody in the grass and I swiftly placed a kick to the center of his eye's, knocking him into the ground. The loud snapping of my foot against his huge cranium was music to my ears and I was laser focused. Duane and I were now ready to fight and just as he leaned towards me, I raised my left leg and smashed his right knee. The force surprised the tall teen, and he went backwards immediately. Grabbing the bat with both hands, Duane enticed his anger with one full swing, and I immediately backed up to avoid the impact. Anyone who has swung a heavy bat realizes the amount of energy it takes and can slow you down in an instant. Duane was winded and just as he fulfilled his swing, I went on the attack.

I once again lunged forward and smashed his right knee with my left foot. The landing was perfect above the kneecap, and he fell to one knee. Just as he looked up at me, I grabbed his afro-looking hair with my left hand and forced my right wrist squarely into the middle of his nose. I repeated the punch twice more and then forced his head against my right knee, knocking him to the ground. Jody appeared to be knocked out and Craig had already run off into the town of Topsfield. Looking down on the coward who was sticking up for his beliefs, he had been defeated with ease. Each punch earlier brought forth the faces of all the bullies at school to the forefront and I pummeled them gracefully. Masco high school embellished their bullies, and I secretly won a war that contained many battles over the years. Duane lay on the ground in the fetal position and that is where I left him. The tenants inside the house started to appear and that is when I took the time to begin riding the bike home.

This was my moment, and it was the revenge I deserved. I was able to kick the shit out of three seniors and this sent a clear message. I was no longer going to be the maggot for these pieces of shit, and I had raised awareness. Whispers throughout town had made it to the hallways of Masco, because apparently a freshman had witnessed the entire fight from her bedroom window. In the days after the incident, the three boys denied their loss to many that surrounded them. Somehow, Jessica was on my mind, and she knew the truth and she may have been smiling for me at some point without showing it.

Bullies had been a staple at Masconomet High School for many years and the faculty was just as much to blame. Principal Anderson professed his power and would possibly destroy any future career I may have had in Baseball. It all came down to this idiot Dwight and his relationship with Brian Woodbury. They conspired together because Brian was a pussy and couldn't handle a small joke in the cafeteria. Was it worth it to Duane to get his ass kicked a few times? Maybe it was and with only a couple of days left of school, Duane would fail to show his face.

The whispers traveled quickly throughout school and people knew better than to fuck with me. Secretly, hundreds of students were thanking what I had done because we were the pulse of the maggots. We were the kids everyone bullied into misery, but it was my stand that created hope. The courage I lent to many was slowly transferring onto the baseball diamond. We were in the State Playoffs and with our first three wins, we would face Salem High School in the State Divisional Finals. With the winner facing a solid Drury team, I was expecting to take my turn in the rotation, knowing Mike was more than likely pitching against us.

"Shawn, I am going with Rick against Salem", Coach Sauchuk stated.

"Coach, are you kidding me right now? Are you trying to lose?" I asked.

"You have walked a few batters the last couple of games, and I think it is best we use Rick, who had a solid game recently", coach replied.

Coach was referring to my game against Bishop Fenwick and my erratic pitching. I had just woken up ill that morning and I chose to pitch anyway. I fared well giving up three hits, but I had walked four batters. We won the game 7-3, but I was off for the first time in a few years, so I understood his position. Rick had escaped barely in our next game against Saugus with a flurry of surrendered hits and untimely runs. He wasn't himself all year and with the help of our bullpen, we escaped with a narrow two run advantage. Several days later, I faced a tough lineup against Stoneham. They had lost two games all season and I had my work cut out for me.

I wasn't sure what was going on in my brain, but I struggled mightily on the mound for the second game in a row. According to the Salem Evening News and the Boston Globe, I was one of a handful of pitchers in the last twenty years to record fifteen strikeouts and seven walks. The strikeouts were across five innings as every single recorded out was a strikeout. My fastball reached as high as ninety miles per hour and my curveball was working to perfection. The walks were attributed to poor umpire play, but we knew it was just part of the game. I should have struck out twenty batters, but the stupid ump behind the plate was blind. I was coloring the black of the plate all day, but he unfortunately wasn't having it. I will never forget what the papers in Boston said about our game. They were nicknaming me Eddie Laloosh from Bull Durham. I wasn't terribly excited about it, but we did win the game 11-2. How the fuck do you walk that many batters and only surrender 1 hit? It was my reality, and we won our way to a date with Salem in the regional finals. A week would pass until our date with infamy and coach wanted to stick with Rick.

A huge part of me found it strange the coach of Salem calling our coach and asking if I would pitch against Mike Girardi. It was the attention we deserved and an epic battle. Salem lost a couple of games that year against Drury and Stoneham, and I was more than capable of beating them.

"Coach, I think it is best for the team if I pitch this game", I stated.

"Shawn, I have the final decision and I think you should sit back and get ready for Drury", he stated.

"Coach, I never really liked you. I think you make horrible decisions and with all due respect. Go fuck yourself and the horse you rode in on", I shouted while walking out of the locker room.

I was done with Masco baseball, and I had every intention of leaving and never returning. I chose my pride over a baseball team that was short of its goal. Our coach had no interest in winning and despite the effort, Masco would get killed by Salem 8-2. Rick lasted a few innings and Salem never relinquished their lead. There is no doubt if I had pitched against Salem and batted in our lineup, we would have easily advanced and won the State Championship that year. Just to prove a point, I would accept a second invite to the Bay State Games in 1990 and place first in the MVP voting. My .650 batting average and twelve strikeouts lead the competition, and I transferred the success into another solid summer in Babe Ruth. Without recourse, I informed the entire team I was moving away to another state. Gary informed our family he was moving us to New Orleans, Louisiana. I wanted desperately to transfer to Salem High School, but this was an out from Masco and its horrific culture.

I could never hate Gary for moving us because I was done with this crappy high school. The principal was crooked, and the faculty were just as bad as the bullies in our school. I probably would have done a lot better for the football program our senior year since they would only win two games our senior year. The baseball team miserably failed to live up to the previous couple of years and the track team would lose a game without me. Masconomet had an exceptional athlete in their midst, and they incorrectly utilized his talents. In the years from 1987-1990 in Babe Ruth Summer baseball, I would average over .675 at the plate. We won four baseball championships, and I would collect 32 wins with one loss. Coincidentally, I would lose in 1990 to a young cocky freshman who reminded myself of someone who pitched against Rick Anthony. He was an electric pitcher named Eric Wainwright and he was just as pushy as I was, and it was fun to be a part of. My career as Masco ended with a measly 19-2 record and a cool 1.85 earned run average. Some of those wins came from my freshman year and I wanted it to correlate into a State Championship. Both years in the Bay State Games competition yielded 2 wins on the mound and a 0.60 earned run average. In the six games at Bay State, my batting average of .712 earned a well-respected visit from professional and college scouts. If Dick Sauchuk had pulled his head out of his ass, I would have more than likely made it professionally in Major League Baseball. Our class was a handful of selected individuals that made it to the state playoffs in back-to-back years. I am fully confident in saying that if I had been put on our batting order those two years in 1989-1990, Masco could have gone down as one of the best teams in the country. I would have helped everyone become better on our team and we would have easily gone 45-1 in those years. Thanks to Dick Sauchuk, he would ruin that chance and decapitate our dreams with relative ease.

I could have easily moved my game to New Orleans and continued my dominance, but good old Gary attempted to bully me during the move. It was the Summer of 1990, and we were relocating to another state and for some reason, he was being a prick. My sister and mother had already relocated to a hotel in the small town of Slidell, Louisiana.

I was left to ponder the abuse for the entire trip from Massachusetts. Hour after hour, this fucking asshole took it upon himself to offer his control for no reason. Maybe he was upset for God knows what, but he demanded perfection upon attending the new High School. I simply had enough of this fucking loser and without hesitation, I told him to fuck himself.

It was a mistake on my part, but he cracked a backhand against my face unexpectedly. I wanted badly to punch him back, but he was driving on the highway, and this was the last straw. Because of his horrific abuse over the many years, I decided to retire completely from high school sports. Slidell High School was going to lose out on a potential All-American, and they can blame Gary Wallis for that shit. This jerk crossed the line too many times and I was completely done. Despite the move and the anxiety coming with the long trip, our family would settle into a new home, a new school and a new life. The year of 1991 was silent, and I was oblivious to the meaning. I would walk away from sports forever and I didn't need my family in my life. I would enter the military and barely speak to Gary for the remainder of the next thirty years and counting.

In the year of 1993, I found myself in the Lynnfield area of Massachusetts and back on a semi-pro team. I can never forget seeing Jeff Milks and a few of my old classmates in the stands. I wasn't duplicating the success I had in high school and the absences were obvious, but I was having fun. I lived on my own, I was balanced, and I was a year away from completely retiring from baseball. A part of me will always live on the diamond and I always second guess what could have happened if I had been a part of the lineup in my sophomore and junior years. I can look in the rear view mirror any time I want, but for once in my life, how I wish I could have seen a part of me staring back. I would always wonder what he would say to me with those devilish blue eyes and anxious lips. Maybe he would convince me to be more assertive or maybe he would tell me to remain silent. Regardless, I washed my hands clean of the mess I became entangled with and watched karma visit me more than once in the future. Masco was left far behind with its bullying and cruel winters. I had taken a valuable lesson with me in life and learned that no matter who chooses to dictate their anger upon me, they would substantially get is much worse.

The End

Letter from the Author

I want to take the time to thank everyone involved that made this all happen. I would throw myself into the fires of hell over and over to garner a story worth writing about. The entire book is based on a true story and if I accidentally left anyone out, then please forgive my early dementia. Masconomet High School was somehow a part of my destiny and when I was nearly killed in 8th grade, I knew the stars would align perfectly when we moved to Topsfield. I would attend Masco High School from 1988-1990 and befriend a few students that were lucky enough to be called friends. I will be honest and admit I was not a fan of the school and its priorities to defend victims of bullying. From what I have seen over the years since,

Masco has done a horrible job in preventing these situations. From my terrible story to many others after, the faculty didn't take the initiative to offer help. I hope this book offers a valuable lesson in those who want to face their bullies. What I went through was both inexcusable and unfortunate. Since I couldn't trust anyone, I fought back in my own way and became successful. Today, I am a business owner, author living in Tampa, Florida and I exhibit my teachings of Kenpo and Aikido irregularly to the local kids of our area. I never heard from the captain again and he will always live in my memory, and I am fortunate to have known him. For most of you who want to know what happened after I moved from Masco, well here goes.

In the spring of 1991, I would move on from Slidell High School in Louisiana and join the US Navy. I had retired from baseball permanently and did not record one more inning until 1993. I would tour the world for a period of two years before leaving the military and moving back to the Boston area. I would play one year of semi-pro ball before venturing to New Orleans. I would delightfully accept a position into a sales company and the rest is history. In 1993, I befriended a few of my younger classmates and I would be arrested for carnal knowledge of a juvenile. I was in a relationship with a beautiful girl by the name of Candie. I was friends with her entire family since I had moved to the Slidell area in 1990. With her mother's blessing, we dated for a while as she was 17. One thing led to another, and I was arrested in August on a criminal complaint I had not committed. I have never been in trouble before with the law and with the good graces of God, Candie's mother would entice the police to let me go without any charges. It was understood that Candie was upset that I had broken up with her and she made up a charge to get me in trouble. I had no business being with her and coincidentally, I would befriend Candie again in 2005 and she apologized for lying. I had forgiven her for what she did and many years later, Candie passed away in her sleep at the age of 33 in 2011. I was glad I was able to make amends when I did, and she earned my forgiveness.

In 2004, I had just broken up with a longtime girlfriend of nine years and introduced myself to internet dating. Wasn't an easy feat and a girl by the name of Leah pounced on me being single. We had a lot of common interests, and we were inseparable for a few months. Upon getting space, I found a link in my computer that brought me to a dating website of Leah's. Since I was able to log in without issue, I discovered several emails between men she had met or slept with. I was dating a serial dater and I immediately stomped that idea right out of my life. I would confront this 24-year-old piece of white trash and boot her to the curb. Apparently, it isn't that easy to break up with a Mississippi girl, because she came at me hard. Her revenge would pin her mother against me, and I was unaware she was friends with the Head Sheriff in St Tammany Parish. Before I knew it, I was being arrested at my job for stalking. Before this goes any further, let me learn you something here. I confronted a cheater, kicked her out of my life and now I am being arrested for stalking. How the fuck is that even possible? Welcome to Louisiana where corruption will protect the crazy women. I immediately bonded out and went back home in my subtle ways. Just when I thought things couldn't get any worse, this bitch's mother calls me at work and tells me no one is going to miss me and that I better run. I didn't consider her words of warning, but I sure did miss the train here. Just as I thought about it, the police arrested me again for the same fucking charge.

No proof, no witnesses, no texts, nothing! I was arrested on two false charges and wait until you hear this. Hurricane Katrina arrived and I suddenly moved to Florida while the case was still pending for a total of ten years. I kid you not and the DA was not dismissing the charges. Despite zero evidence, the Sheriff advised the DA to continue holding this over my head. My lawyer and I decided to plea to a misdemeanor, since this was never going away. The plea would haunt me years later, but we will get to that. Coincidentally in 2018, that same Sheriff (Jack Strain) was arrested and convicted of rape, incest, sexual battery and indecent behavior. This classless piece of shit used his power to abuse his own family members and finally got caught. He was a sick fuck and he deserved what he had coming, and my prayers were answered. Today, I retained counsel and have filed a dismissal of my accepted plea, since the Sheriff was directly involved.

Unfortunately, I was able to date a few women here and there and ran across a psychotic woman by the name of Brenda St Martin. That name will ring significant because she wasn't the typical woman I would seek. I had seen her briefly before I met Leah and upon understanding her drug habit, I dismissed her rather quickly. Since this idiot befriended my sister, I would have to deal with this person for a very long time and her harassment. If we counted today (2022), Brenda has been stalking me for well over 18 years. Swallow that and tell me if you can beat it? Bullies can come in many ways from female to males and it can happen at any time or even over a couple of decades. Maybe the girl never got over me letting her go, but whatever the case may be, no one deserves that type of treatment.

Living in Florida was not easy. I was estranged because of Hurricane Katrina and moved here on a whim without anything to call my own. I had to start over once more in life and with a little patience, good luck, and a new wife, I was back on my feet. Her name was Susan, and she had a young nine-year-old daughter. The marriage lasted longer than a Chinese Christmas, and that is giving it too much credit. Without remorse, I moved fifty miles away to the town of Brandon, Florida in 2009. For the first time in my life, I was living near a mall, and I was fucking happier than a pig in shit. I left my wife, my job and my friends to start over again in another town, and this almost became the norm. In a span of a few years, I had moved three times and the adversity strengthened me.

I was in a new apartment, new life and things were changing. I found a new job as a store manager in the automotive repair industry, my stalker lost her control and I found someone new. From 2011-2012, I would experience heartbreak like no other. I found two women that took my heart and gobbled it into a million pieces, without blinking an eye. I made the improbable mistake of allowing two females to rupture the foundation I had built. Since I was distraught, I befriended a woman by the name of Justine Burke through a Christian dating site. The purpose was to make a friend or two, and it worked to perfection. Unaware of her bi-polar diagnosis, we became roommates in the town of Brandon in 2012. We decided to live in luxury and rented a beautiful condo off a beautiful lake. We both redecorated and it was a beautiful masterpiece, but it surrounded the fakeness of someone I had despised immediately. Justine was from Boston and her red hair was as spicy as her demeanor. I had possibly made a deal with the devil and my life would nearly turn upside down in an instant.

On November 24th, 2013, the New England Patriots were hosting Peyton Manning's Denver Broncos on Sunday night football. It was an amazing game, and since I was earlier diagnosed with Prolymphocytic T-Cell Leukemia, I wasn't feeling well. My temperature was through the roof, and I needed Advil to help fight my inner issues. I was sleeping in the spare bedroom and Justine was a die-hard Patriots fan. She was screaming loud, and I couldn't take the noise since my head was ready to explode. Normally, Justine was taking care of me as my friend and making sure I was taking my medicine and putting ice packs on my head when I was running a fever. The Lemtrada I was taking for my Leukemia relegated me radioactive at times, and I felt like a microwave. The pain was unbearable, and I was glad the vomiting only lasted a day or sometimes two. The fever would take over for the next several days and how I was able to work through it all, was amazing.

I wasn't diagnosed right away, and it took my death to realize there was something terribly wrong. It was March 30th, 2013, and I was unable to eat anything a month prior. I had rapidly lost weight and my health was failing miserably. I was tired, somber and barely able to function, but since my store was having a record month, I couldn't miss the action. The pain subsiding throughout my limbs was a daily occurrence and nothing in the world would help. I was drinking water, but I just couldn't eat. I had thought breaking up with a girl the month before was the sole reason for my health. Since March was at its end, I was nearly 60 pounds lighter, and I drove home that afternoon.

My assistant manager was concerned and called the sheriffs office when I left. I was not right, and I could barely envision the road, let alone drive in a straight line. Somehow and someway, I made it to my home fifteen minutes away and passed out in my garage. Flatlining twice on the way to the hospital, I drifted into a three-day long coma and a whole new adventure began. I would pen the book, *The Devil in Polo* a couple of years later. It would entail my journey during those three days I was relegated to a hospital bed and left comatose. I thought I was dying and with the help of the hospital staff, they kept me alive in time to learn that I needed to see an Oncologist. It was a couple of months later I would be diagnosed with Leukemia and my fight enraged on. Despite the illness, I was now 165 pounds and at the same weight in high school. I was looking good, but the chemotherapy pill was preventing me from sleeping. I looked like a zombie and my daily routines were interrupted without blinking twice.

Going back to the night of that Patriots game, I was at a loss. I was woken up by Justine's happiness over the comeback by Tom Brady. I was seeking solace in the form of a small pill, and I was unable to locate any. Justine had informed me they were in her dresser drawer by the bed, and I could help myself. Without hesitation, I began digging under the massive papers, and that is when I located a large white envelope from a doctor. It was strange, because it was torn open, and I invited myself to the results. In the upper corner of the paperwork, the numbers were jumbled since my brain was on fire. Focusing a little more, I noticed next to the letters, HIV, the word, positive. Thinking for a second, Justine had been acting weird for a while. The date of the paperwork was stamped in May of 2013, and she had been hiding her diagnosis for a long while. I sat with my hands on my head wondering what I just read, and to be sure, I asked her to come into the room.

"Hey, did you find those pills?" She asked as she pierced through the door.

"Justine, I have not. But can you explain this test here please?" I asked with concern.

"Oh no. You weren't supposed to find that. I can explain", she offered.

Justine told me she had missed her period by two months and thought she was pregnant with her boyfriend's child. She tested positive on her home pregnancy test, so she was inclined to check herself into the Doctor's office. Not only was she not pregnant, but she tested positive for HIV. Clueless and distraught, she kept the news to herself, and failed to tell anyone at work, her friends or myself and her daughter. Living life abnormally for the last several months, I recall Justine becoming frisky with me one night.

"Justine, you tried to have sex with me. You could have infected me months ago", I yelled.

"I know and I wicked sorry. You turned me down and you didn't get anything. Why are you so upset?" She asked frantically.

Justine didn't understand that she could have infected me, so the first thing I did was tell her I was leaving. I was cone with her bullshit, her lies and the manipulation. Nothing was holding me there and just as I was packing a suitcase, her bi-polar disorder took over.

"Shawn, you are not leaving me. Please don't go", she stated.

"Justine, this I don't want to be your roommate anymore. I can't trust you", I explained.

Just as I turned around to continue packing, Justine yelled out a loud scream and picked up the cable box remote and threw it in my direction.

With no place to land except my face, the remote punctured my brow and opened a large cut above my left eye. My face was on fire, my body was in bad shape and my head was killing me. I was now bleeding from my face and the blood drifted slowly into my eye, blinding me temporarily. I knelt on the ground and Justine's daughter walked into the room and began screaming. With the large amount of blood dripping from my hands as I was covering my face, she thought her mother shot me.

Without a word, Sarah called the police and within minutes, the dispatcher had rushed a few cars over to assist. When the doorbell rang, I could barely focus as Justine was in the middle of several guns pointed at her face. While I lay on the side of the bed covered in my own blood, I began throwing up profusely. This was nothing new, but the police assumed Justine poisoned me. I wasn't a fan of the police in our town and when they had her handcuffed and sitting on the couch, the interviews began for us both. In the end, I would relegate myself to a spineless wimp and ask the police to let her go. If her employer had found out she was arrested for domestic violence with injury, she would have been fired. I wasn't in position to care for her teen daughter, so I gracefully asked them to let her go. Unaware of Florida and its laws, one of us would have to go to jail since it was a domestic violence incident. Being the good man I was, I elected to be handcuffed and placed in the patrol car. It was I who stood up and became charged with battery and visited jail that evening. What I thought was going to be a few our visit, turned into nearly forty-eight hours. Apparently, Florida law also dictated the right to hold a person in jail for twenty-four hours as a cool-off period. I couldn't argue with the law and Justine took the initiative to immediate have the charges dropped.

The day I came home was the last day I would see Justine in her apartment. We agreed to let her keep my furniture temporarily as I would move away and live on my own with friends. It would be a year later and no contact with

Justine when I received the stupid order of protection. Justine was upset that I was collecting my furniture and she filed a fake restraining order to prevent me from retrieving my belongings. With relative ease, the judge in the case threw the order away as fast as we attended court. He wasn't happy with Justine and her antics, and I can confidently say I never saw her again and never wanted too. For someone to try and affect my health with her disease was infallible and I never forgave her for that. To make matters worse, she would call my sister and my employer and tell them I had HIV. My sister was stupid enough to tell her friends and this allowed her psychotic friend Brenda to harass me for many years later. Justine had started the false rumor and she assumed she gave me her disease. Justine was served with a cease and desist and to date, I have never heard from that piece of shit in over eight years and counting. Once in a while over the years, I would see Justine on the news helping the community with her projects at Metropolitan Ministries. Even then, all I can think about is the deadly disease she carries and how she could have avoided it all. She wasn't perfect, but somehow, I felt terrible because if I had never met her, we would not be where we are today.

I would find love once again in the form of a woman who was now reading one of my books. *The Devil in Polo* was a popular book on Amazon reaching #2 on September 16, 2014, in sales. Also, Barnes and Noble would report the book as one of it best selling books in the same time period. That is a huge misconception of the name, "Best Seller". People tend to think the book was on the New York Times Best Sellers list and that is clearly not the case. The several books I have written over the many years, a few select novels have become best selling on Amazon, Walmart or Barnes & Nobles. Those statistics are relative to the daily sales, since they are measured hourly. I was lucky enough to find one of my novels ranked #5 in Europe back in 2018 on Amazon.

BESTSELLER NO. 5

A Beautiful Lie
Shawn Wallis

A Beautiful Lie (English Edition)

🛒 Acquista su Amazon

A stranger by the name of Becky would entice my interest and she was enthused by my books. This interest would turn into a friendship, and I would marry her in December of 2015. I made a conscientious decision to marry someone I didn't know and the day before the wedding, Brenda St Martin took the initiative to email Becky on Facebook.

Brenda stated that I was not a good person, and I would cheat on Becky, and I had HIV since 2004. The entire message was immature, and you could tell some trailer trash moron authored its rhetoric. I was surprised that someone was jealous of what I had in my life and anyone with common sense saw the desperation. Becky immediately dismissed it as a weak person with no life and we were married the following day. In all honesty, I wish she had called the wedding off because it began a three-year prison term. Becky had married me for money, and she was about to dry me out as fast as she could. The liquid I inherited from my books, my large salary and my savings account were invitations for her to be in my life. When I finally convinced myself to cut her off financially, Becky would take it upon herself to open four credit card accounts under my name in 2016 and 2017. Unaware of her crimes, she began possessing new items that were explained as gifts or prizes from work. She was the new owner of a treadmill, office equipment, bikes, kitchen set, and many other valuable assets.

I would validate her reasons and not think twice about it. I wasn't paying for them, and I had no reason to believe they had anything to do with me. The cat was let out of the bag when we both decided a divorce was the correct decision as a family. I was done with the relationship and when I moved into my own place, several months would pass and the collections started rolling in. Since I was unaware of the issues on my credit, I soon realized I was in trouble when I applied for a new credit card. My credit score was in the toilet and when I realized who was behind it all, I notified the local authorities.

Becky had run up nearly $20,000 in debt under my name and I was left wondering why. The police informed me since we were married, the issue would have to be resolved in civil court. For the next few years, I would be fighting the credit bureaus and filing reports of identity theft. It was a mess and despite the anger, I proceeded to allow another woman in my life for fun.

I was not interested in a relationship and a young customer named Michelle decided she would aggressively pursue me. If you ever read the book, *The Devil in Polo Returns*, it entails the horrific crimes she would commit during and after we met. This twenty something year-old young mother of three was a temporary stay in my life and since I was still in the middle of a divorce, it was my reality. I was thinking she attempted to garner more than I could offer and when I ceased to see her anymore, she took it upon herself to abuse and nearly kill my eight-week-old puppy. In June of 2019, I was suddenly arrested for stalking this piece of shit. This vixen would dig into my past on the internet for the next thirty days after I left her. She would eventually find the case against me in Louisiana, and she did the unthinkable. This psychotic idiot walked into the Zephyrhills Police Department with my previous case in hand, and claimed I did the same exact things to her. Literally, you cannot make this cruel shit up. The unoriginal material was boring, and she stated I was stalking her with a little evidence she brought with her. She would claim that I was emailing her, texting her and without remorse, she was serious as a heart attack. The worst I had done was call this puppy-abusing loser on the phone and left a nasty voicemail. The worst kind of woman in the world to fuck with is one that will ruin your life over breaking up. Well, this fancy Nancy found it reasonable in her psychotic mind to falsify emails and conjure up evidence to convince the police I was a stalker. Failing to return my borrowed iPad, this idiot would break into my emails, my amazon account, my bank account, and my life and conjure up days of conversations.

Moving forward, the Judge and I agreed the wrong person was prosecuted and I mildly agreed to the charges to move my life beyond harm. I was jailed for literally ten minutes and my life did not skip a beat. Here is where the strange gets stranger. You would think the arrest would allow this piece of shit to move on and bother someone else. Well, you would be wrong because this whack job stalked me every day since I left her. She would make fake profiles on Facebook and then post awful things to get my attention. Just before you think this could worse, it did.

Jamie Sullivan
5m

Your life is so sad. I almost feel bad for you. Almost. Try defending yourself all you want, but no arrest would've been made without proof and I made sure of that. Not my fault the Zephyrhills Police are stupid in the evidence I gave them. How awesome is it that they didn't believe you when I hurt Samantha? I am laughing at you Shawn Wallis. I did this to you asshole and there isn't one thing you can do to me. The fact that you think you're innocent is fucking hysterical. You had a good life with me and you went and fucked it all up with that fucking dumb puppy. The fact that you think a so-called "abused puppy" is the reason Florida changed their animal abuse laws is absurd. Do some research before you spew blatant lies. No laws were changed because of YOUR stupid dog, especially considering you had no proof. If you had proof, I would've had charges filed against me. Fyi, it helps when I am fucking one of the cops. Just saying! How are you this stupid? Is it painful to be so fucking dumb that I own your fucking ass?

All of the reviews about your horrendous books are from people you know. When you can't even use proper grammar on the back cover summary. The fact that you use so many lies to hype up your shitty life must be a sad way to live. How pathetic that you spoil your dogs. No one gives a shit about your dogs, don't you understand that? You whine and cry about how many women have cheated on you. Get over it, man. Grow up. You're almost 50 and still single and childless because NO ONE WANTS YOU 😂😂 At least the one lady was smart enough to abort your child. I commend her!

I get to move on to West Palm Beach with a nice new promotion and happy, healthy children and a husband while you stay stuck in your boring,

how many women have cheated on you. Get over it, man. Grow up. You're almost 50 and still single and childless because NO ONE WANTS YOU 😂😂 At least the one lady was smart enough to abort your child. I commend her!
I get to move on to West Palm Beach with a nice new promotion and happy, healthy children and a husband while you stay stuck in your boring, uneventful, shitty life. Who's jealous now? You could have been a part of this, but you had to dump me. Did you learn your fucking lesson?
I sincerely hope you enjoy being a worthless nothing human being who gets all of their self esteem and validation from posting lies about their life on social media because no one on there knows you enough to know it's all bullshit. Even going as far as to put yourself in relationships with fake people and commenting on your own statuses as them. Must be a severely lonely life! I take huge comfort in knowing you will die knowing your life was full of lies, and knowing you had nothing in this world. I should have shot you the night I was in the parking lot watching you get arrested because of me. I want you to know that I was in your condo when you were taken away that night and I stole your money out of the cash jar. Oh, I also kicked Samantha as hard as I could and she cried. The universe was speaking when it knew not to allow your spawn to enter this world. Biohazard waste bucket was the perfect place for it. 😊
And btw, "TBT" stands for "throwback Thursday", so please stop using verbiage you don't know the meaning of. Posting old photos on a random day of the week tagging it "TBT" - what a fucking tool. 😂
#samanthastrong #madisonstrong #sorrynotsorry #weimaranerdiaries #thedevilinpolo

This dumb fuck moved her bastard kids and herself into a condo next to me. Did I just say that? The woman who spilled her guts to the police and claimed she was afraid of me, moved into the same community next door. Why in the world would someone do that unless they were psychotic? This was my world, and I didn't change one thing because I was still in control.

Why would someone resort to the lies and stalking of a person who doesn't want you anymore? She was a very dangerous person and since I stopped talking to her in 2019, she made it clear she wasn't over our relationship.

I always knew my past will catch the attention of anyone looking to penetrate my inner circle. I have been either been arrested for things I haven't done, or I kindly offered my freedom to help someone else in need. Either way, I am proud of everything I have done to this point because my stalkers will never be satisfied. Regardless of their lives, I will never forget why these desperate losers need me in their focus. I will always draw their attention because their misery needs the company of something they dearly miss. Since I met Brenda in 2004, I can easily say with confidence I have accumulated over fifteen stalkers.

Despite the large number, Brenda and Michelle have been my largest supporters of my fan club. Regardless of their false innuendos and smear campaigns, they have helped me see a lot of books. I realize their insane rhetoric has attracted some of my old high school classmates and former girlfriends, but nobody is perfect. I am confident these morons will continue to stalk me, and I welcome it. Every fan club needs a following and it is gladly appreciative.

The one thing I regret the most is not disowning my family many years ago. As you read in this book, Gary Wallis literally attempted to kill me several times. I am a survivor of domestic violence, and I am proud to say he is no longer a part of my life. I have never been interested in who my real father is, but I am quite sure I was stolen or misplaced in the Miami Hospital in 1973. I look nothing like my mother, or my sister and I am 1000% sure I belong to another family. The way my parents have acted over the years, it is easy to say that my family tree grows from another garden. I am nearly fifty years old, and I could care less who my real family is at this point.

Because I have recently disowned them, Mandy has taken it upon herself to recruit several people from my past. My sister has stalked and destroyed so many people, it's a wonder how she isn't in prison. She took it upon herself to stalk and prance on one of her neighbors for many years because she endured attention. Her retched behavior would cause this neighbor's husband to be imprisoned for a period of three years, ripping the family apart. Did Mandy stop after that? No, she did not, and she would call the police on that family several more times. I witnessed the behavior against this neighbor for years and I never agreed because I thought it was pointless and sad. She was my sister, so I supported whatever she needed as she victimized this family. When the day came for the husband to be released from jail, Mandy took it upon herself to ask me to conjure up evidence to put him back in prison. She was willing to destroy this family even further and that is when I disowned Mandy.

Since that day in 2022, I have had nothing but issues with Mandy and her unwanted attention. She would conjure false and nasty rumors online and spread them to my old high school for the students to read. What tickles me the most about Mandy is that she is completely in the dark. What made her think I liked that school or wanted to ever be a part of it after I left? I couldn't leave Masco fast enough and for her to throw a lasso over an expectation, was laughable. She had no clue and it made it clear to me that disowning her was the correct move. She was mirroring the same behavior at me like she had with her neighbor, and it was a rerun I didn't have time to watch. Over the many years, I have seen that girl ruin many lives and friendships because of her tendency for control. She is the type of girl that sits in her window in her neighborhood and calls the cops when you are out of line. She is referred to as a "Karen" and that will forever be her staple. Not only is she fake, but than she took the initiative to befriend my puppy's abuser. It was the straw that broke the camel's back, and I took a huge stance. In the past, I would confront my bullies and easily demolish them with a fury of revenge.

Today, it's just easier to walk into a courtroom and hit your bully financially, and that is what I have accomplished. There is no way I can let someone spread false rumors of HIV or lie to the world about me and get away with it.

As of December 2022, I have sought monies from my fake parents and my sister for mental anguish, abuse and stalking. The many years I had to endure their shit are over and it is time I took a stance and fought back. Will it be successful? Yeah sure, but at least I can say I tried and equaled the same effort I made all those years ago. My bullies in High School and today are the same people and all they ever wanted was to improve their own shitty lives.

Take my advice and understand if you are a bullying victim, take a stance. I stood up to my bullies and they paid a huge price years ago. Today, I am standing up to a different kind of bully that hides behind a keyboard and exuberates control within their own minds. Those are the people we face today and let me say this last thing. Bullying is never alright and if you are a victim, find help and call someone and talk about it. Just remember one thing here. Bullies hate their lives, and they harass others because they need control. Take their control from them and watch them wither away like I did.

I am far from perfect, and I have been a victim of child abuse and many other forms of abuse over a thirty to forty-year period. Has it affected me? Sure, it has and no one on Earth is going to convince me that I may be a little screwed up over it. I have never laid my hands on any woman in my entire life and despite what my stalkers have said, that's my final word. I have been arrested falsely a few times in my life and I chalk it up as adversity.

Thanks for reading my incredible story and today I am happily engaged to an amazing woman named Rebecca. Winners win and losers will always lose in the end and despite the adversity, my patience outweighs others ignorance.

Victory is bittersweet!

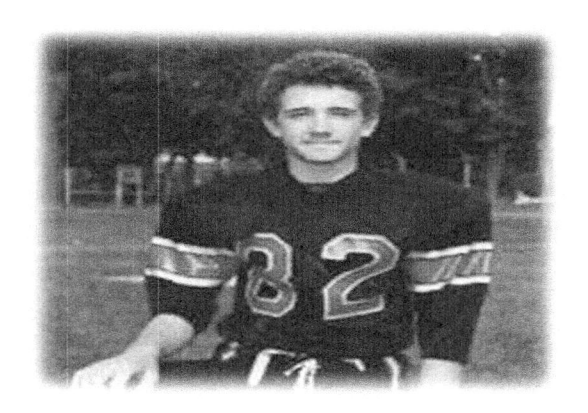

"Victory at all costs, victory in spite of all terror, victory however long and hard the road may be; for without victory, there is no survival."

– Winston Churchill

(Rebecca, Samantha & Madison 2021) (Shawn & Rebecca 2021)

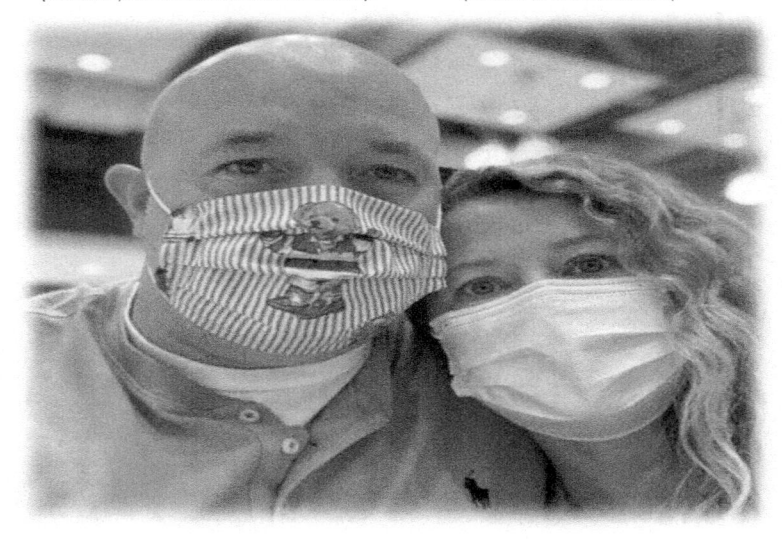

(Rebecca & Shawn 2022)   (Rebecca, Madison & Samantha)

If you are a victim of bullying or have thoughts of suicide, it is never too late to ask for help. Stop bullying today!

SUICIDE PREVENTION
YOU ARE NOT ALONE

Text "Help" to 741-741
24/7 Crisis Text Line: 741-741

Or Call:
1-800-273-TALK (8255)
Suicidepreventionlifeline.org

Newport-Mesa
Unified School District

Copyright © 2022   Shawn Wallis
All rights reserved.